EVERYDAY ITALIAN FAVORITES

RECIPES FOR
DELICIOUS WEEKNIGHT MEALS

EVERYDAY
ITALIAN
FAVORITES

ACADEMIA
BARILLA

RECIPES FOR
DELICIOUS WEEKNIGHT MEALS

The Taunton Press

Original edition © 2014 by De Agostini Libri S.p.A.

The Taunton Press, Inc.
63 South Main Street
PO Box 5506, Newtown, CT 06470-5506
e-mail: tp@taunton.com

Translations:

Irina Oryshkevich - Catherine Howard - Rosetta Translations SARL - Mary Doyle
- John Venerella - Rosetta Translations SARL - Free z'be, Paris - Salvatore Ciolfi -
Contextus s.r.l., Pavia - Helen Farrell

LIBRARY OF CONGRESS CATALOGING-IN-PUBLICATION DATA IN PROGRESS
ISBN: 978-1-62710-709-9

Printed in China
10 9 8 7 6 5 4 3 2 1

EDITED BY
ACADEMIA BARILLA

INTRODUCTION
GIANLUIGI ZENTI

TEXT
LORENA CARRARA
CHEF MARIO GRAZIA
MARIAGRAZIA VILLA

RECIPES
CHEF MARIO GRAZIA

PHOTOGRAPHS
CHEF MARIO GRAZIA
CHEF STEFANO LODI
CHEF MATTEO MANFERDINI
CHATO MORANDI
ALBERTO ROSSI
LUCIO ROSSI
CHEF LUCA ZANGA

ACADEMIA BARILLA EDITORIAL COORDINATION
CHATO MORANDI
REBECCA PICKRELL
ILARIA ROSSI

GRAPHIC DESIGN
MARIA CUCCHI

CONTENTS

LIST OF RECIPES

AN "ITALIAN-STYLE" MEAL

ITALIAN CUISINE REIGNS AS "QUEEN" OF MEDITERRANEAN CUISINES. IN ADDITION TO ITS WEALTH OF AG-RICULTURAL LAND, ITALY HAS A UNIQUE HISTORY WHICH MADE THE COUNTRY'S GASTRONOMY (ESPECIALLY IN THE SOUTHERN REGIONS) HETEROGENEOUS, MULTIFACETED, DIVERSE, AND CAPABLE OF COUNTLESS VARIATIONS ON A RELATIVELY LIMITED RANGE OF PRODUCTS.

LOVE FOR FOOD, RESPECT FOR THE LAND, IMAGINATION, AND THE ABILITY TO UTILIZE EVERY TASTE AND INGREDIENT TO ITS FULLEST POTENTIAL—THESE ELEMENTS WERE SOLIDIFIED OVER CENTURIES, GIVING RISE TO A CULTURAL AND MATERIAL TREASURE TROVE OF RECIPES, TRADITIONAL PRODUCTS, AND DELICACIES.

IT'S CLEAR THAT CHOOSING A DIET IN KEEPING WITH THE MEDITERRANEAN MODEL AND ADOPTING A HEALTHIER LIFESTYLE CAN NOT ONLY LESSEN THE RISK OF DEVELOPING EVEN THE MOST DANGEROUS DISEASES, BUT IT OFFERS YOU FOOD WITH INCREDIBLE TASTE AND AESTHETIC APPEAL. THE MEDITERRANEAN DIET HAS GREAT POTENTIAL FOR DIVERSITY AND ALLOWS FOR A WIDE RANGE OF COOKING METHODS AND COMBINATIONS OF COLORS, TEXTURES, AND FRAGRANCES. IT'S EASILY ADAPTED TO INDIVIDUAL TASTES AND BRINGS EXCITEMENT AND JOY TO THE TABLE. IT ALSO PROVIDES A WAY TO DISCOVER NEW FLAVORS OR REDISCOVER ANCIENT ONES. THE BEST PART IS THAT IT CAN BE FOLLOWED AND REINTERPRETED ALMOST ANYWHERE IN THE WORLD.

THE BASIC MODEL IS VERY SIMPLE AND FLEXIBLE: A BASE OF GRAINS (PREFERABLY WHOLE GRAINS, WHICH

CAN BE EATEN SIMPLY STEAMED OR IN THE FORM OF PASTA, BREAD, POLENTA, OR COUSCOUS) IS COMBINED WITH GENEROUS AMOUNTS OF SEASONAL FRUITS AND VEGETABLES. THIS CAN BE ENHANCED WITH A MODEST QUANTITY OF DAIRY PRODUCTS, EGGS, FISH, MEAT (PREFERABLY LEAN) OR LEGUMES (A GREAT SOURCE OF VEGETABLE PROTEIN). SMALL QUANTITIES OF DRIED FRUIT CAN ALSO BE INCLUDED TO ADD FLAVOR AND NUTRITIONAL VALUE TO CERTAIN DISHES. FINALLY, EXTRA-VIRGIN OLIVE OIL IS THE UNDISPUTED LEADER OF CONDIMENTS AND FATS FOR COOKING.

AN "ITALIAN-STYLE" MEAL IS RICH NOT ONLY FOR THESE REASONS BUT ALSO FOR THE HISTORICAL SIGNIFICANCE THE DISHES POSSESS. THIS BOOK UNITES A SELECTION OF THE BEST RECIPES—TRADITIONAL, CONTEMPORARY, AND ENTIRELY MEDITERRANEAN—WITH IN-DEPTH EXPLANATIONS OF THEIR HISTORY AND IMPORTANCE BEYOND MERELY A TASTE PROFILE. SCIENCE MAY HAVE PROVEN THE NUTRITIONAL VALUE OF THE MEDITERRANEAN DIET, BUT REDISCOVERING LOCAL RECIPES WITHOUT KNOWLEDGE OF THEIR ROOTS, OR CHOOSING THEM FOR NUTRITIONAL REASONS ALONE, WOULD BE ONLY HALF THE STORY. THE TEACHINGS OF THE PAST ALLOW US TO GRASP THE MEANING OF A TRADITION, TO FOLLOW IT, AND TO REINTERPRET IT, ADAPTING IT TO THE TIMES WE LIVE IN. AFTER ALL, THE HISTORY OF THE MEDITERRANEAN AND ITS EXTRAORDINARY GASTRONOMIC CULTURE IS STILL BEING MADE TODAY.

STARTERS

CHAPTER ONE

BAKED PARMIGIANO REGGIANO WITH TRUFFLES

PARMIGIANO REGGIANO AL FORNO CON TARTUFO

Preparation time: 10 minutes + 3 minutes cooking time

4 Servings

5 oz. (150 g) **Parmigiano Reggiano cheese (about 1 1/2 cups)**
1 1/2 tbsp. (20 g) **unsalted butter**
1 **medium truffle, shaved**

Method

Heat the oven to 350°F (175°C). Using a vegetable peeler, shave the Parmigiano into very thin slices.

Generously butter four ramekins. Place a slice of the Parmigiano in each. Add a sliver of truffle, then top with another slice of Parmigiano. Continue to layer the Parmigiano and truffle (ending with the cheese) in this manner until all the ingredients have been used.

Bake until the Parmigiano begins to melt, about 3 minutes. Serve immediately.

Did you know that...

Parmigiano Reggiano cheese and truffles, two indisputable champions of Italian gastronomic culture, are exquisite flavors that go together perfectly, especially in dishes that are very simple, such as this recipe for fried eggs: Separate two eggs. Whip the egg whites in a bowl until they're frothy. Fry them in a skillet with a drizzle of olive oil. When they are almost done cooking, add the two yolks to the middle of the frying whites, cooking only long enough so that the yolks remain soft. Remove the eggs from the heat, scatter a few flakes of Parmigiano Reggiano and slivers of truffle over the top, season with salt, and serve very hot.

Difficulty

RICE FRITTERS

ARANCINI

Preparation time: 30 minutes + 20 minutes cooking time

4 Servings

3 cups (3/4 l) **beef broth**
1 1/3 cups (250 g) **rice**
3 **large eggs**
2 tbsp. (30 g) **unsalted butter**
1/3 cup plus 1 tbsp. (40 g) **grated Parmigiano Reggiano cheese**
3 1/2 oz. (100 g) **smoked Scamorza or smoked mozzarella cheese, diced small**
3/4 cup plus 1 tbsp. (100 g) **all-purpose flour**
1 3/4 cups plus 1 tbsp. (200 g) **breadcrumbs**
3 1/2 oz. (100 g) **crushed hazelnuts (about 1 cup)**
Olive oil for frying, as needed

Method

In a large saucepan, bring the broth to a boil. Add the rice and simmer until the rice is cooked al dente, about 15 minutes. Drain the rice in a fine-mesh sieve and transfer to a large bowl.

Stir in 1 egg, the butter, and the Parmigiano and let the rice mixture cool.

Form the rice mixture into balls (about the size of Ping-Pong balls), placing a piece of Scamorza or mozzarella in the center of each one.

Place the flour in a medium bowl. In another bowl, stir together the breadcrumbs and hazelnuts. Lightly beat the remaining 2 eggs in a third bowl. Coat the rice balls in flour, then dip them in the beaten egg and coat them in the breadcrumb mixture.

Heat 1 1/2 inches (4 cm) of oil in a 4-quart (3 1/2 l) heavy pot over moderately high heat until it registers 365°F (185°C) on an instant-read or candy thermometer, then lower the rice balls into the oil and fry in batches, stirring occasionally, until golden, about 3 minutes per batch.

With a slotted spoon, transfer the fritters to paper towels to drain before serving.

Difficulty

CHICKPEA FLATBREAD

FARINATA

Preparation time: 15 minutes + 12 hours resting time + 20 minutes cooking time

4 Servings

3 1/2 cups (400 g) **chickpea flour**
4 cups (950 ml) **water**
**Salt and freshly ground black pepper
  to taste**
1/2 cup (118 ml) **extra-virgin olive oil**

Method

In a large bowl, whisk together the chickpea flour and the 4 cups of water. Season with salt and allow to rest for 12 hours. Skim off any froth that has formed on the surface, then stir the flour mixture.

Heat the oven to 425°F (220°C). Prepare a large rimmed baking sheet by drizzling the olive oil to coat the bottom.

Pour the batter through a fine-mesh sieve onto the pan, making a layer about 1/4 inch (6 1/2 mm) deep. Stir the batter with a wooden spoon to absorb the oil. Sprinkle generously with pepper.

Bake for about 20 minutes, or until golden-brown. Serve warm.

Did you know that...

Farinata is a chickpea-based focaccia that is typical of the city of Genoa. In 1284, a Genoese ship was returning from the victorious battle of Meloria, against the fleet of Pisa, when it got caught in a storm. The storage room of the ship had been stocked with chickpeas and other provisions, and after the storm passed, the sailors checked to see what was left of their supplies. Apparently, salt water had seeped into the storage room, creating a sort of chickpea purée. Having nothing else to eat, the sailors fed themselves the mush, which, in the heat of the sun, had turned into a sort of bread, and was extremely tasty. Once they reached land, they decided to replicate the dish, calling it farinata.

Difficulty

ANCHOVIES IN A VINEGAR MARINADE

SCAPECE DE LICETTE

Preparation time: 45 minutes + 15 minutes cooking time

4 Servings

1 lb. (500 g) **fresh young anchovies**
3/4 cup plus 1 tbsp. (100 g)
  all-purpose flour
Vegetable oil, for frying
Salt to taste
5 **fresh sage leaves**
1 **clove garlic, chopped**
2 cups (450 g) **white wine vinegar**
1 cup **water**

Method

Rinse and drain the anchovies gently in a colander. Coat the anchovies in flour.

In a skillet, heat 1/2 inch (1 cm) of oil until it is shimmering. Fry the anchovies until they are golden. With a slotted spoon, transfer them to paper towels to drain. Salt to taste. Arrange the anchovies in a glass or ceramic salad bowl, sprinkling each layer with sage leaves and chopped garlic.

In a large pan, bring the vinegar, water, and a pinch of salt to a boil. Let the marinade cool slightly (it should still be hot but not boiling). Pour over the anchovies. Cover and let rest in the marinade for a few days (that is when they taste best).

Young anchovies—to be eaten whole—are only available in spring, and are not readily available in the U.S. You can substitute baby sardines, if you like.

Did you know that...

Food preparation doesn't necessarily mean cooking, even in the Italian tradition, and marinating is one example. A marinade is a sort of sauce in which foods are left to soak for a long time, sometimes for a whole day. The presence of acidic ingredients (vinegar, citrus juices or alcoholic beverages) transforms the flavor, consistency and appearance of the food so that it's almost been "cold-cooked." This process is typical of Italian gastronomy, whether it's merely the preliminary phase of a more complicated recipe or simply a single food preparation step. It's a very ancient method that was created to extend the shelf life of food items, but it continues to be part of the Mediterranean tradition today because of its irrefutable value in terms of taste and nutrition.

Difficulty

TOMATO-BASIL BRUSCHETTA

BRUSCHETTA CON POMODORO E BASILICO

Preparation time: 20 minutes

4 Servings

1 **baguette (about 1 lb., or 500 g)**
1 **clove garlic**
11 oz. (300 g) **tomatoes, preferably San Marzano (about 1 1/2 large), diced**
1 1/2 tbsp. (20 ml) **extra-virgin olive oil**
Salt to taste
4 **fresh basil leaves, chopped**

Method

Cut the baguette into 1/2-inch (1 cm) thick slices. Toast them in the oven under the broiler for a couple of minutes on each side, or in a skillet set over medium heat.

Peel the garlic and lightly rub it over the toasted bread. Place the tomatoes in a bowl and season them with the oil, salt, and basil. Let the tomato mixture sit for a few minutes to allow the flavors to blend. Spread the tomato mixture evenly over the toast and serve.

Did you know that...

In the past, many people made their bread at home using coarsely ground whole grain flours and natural yeast made through a long and precise treatment applied to already leavened bread. The bacteria responsible for this leavening gave the bread an unmistakable aroma. And the higher acidity of starters, compared to modern yeast, made the bread more resistant to further contamination by bacteria and therefore made it more "preservable," which is why bread once lasted much longer. This would be enough to explain why loaves of rustic country bread could be so incredibly large, but there are other factors that played into the size and shape of bread. First there were socio-economic factors. If farming families had their own oven, or there was one easily accessible to the collective, the bread was smaller. On the contrary, when the powerful were in charge of the ovens, more loaves were baked, in a way making the family more autonomous with respect to the local lords.

Difficulty

SAVORY TOMATO AND GOAT CHEESE TORTA

CROSTATA AL POMODORO E CAPRINO

Preparation time: 20 minutes + 30 minutes cooking time

4 Servings

7 oz. (200 g) **puff pastry**
  (about 1 sheet)
7 oz. (200 g) **tomatoes**
  (about 2 small), sliced
2 oz. (60 g) **goat cheese, sliced**
1 tsp. **cornstarch**
2/3 cup (150 ml) **lukewarm milk**
1 **large egg**
2 1/2 tbsp. (15 g) **grated**
  Parmigiano Reggiano cheese
1 **bunch fresh chives, chopped**
Salt and freshly ground black pepper
  to taste

Method

Heat the oven to 350°F (175°C).

On a clean work surface, roll out the puff pastry to about 1/8 inch (3 mm) thick. Line a 9-inch (23 cm) baking pan or 4 ramekins with the pastry.

Arrange the sliced tomatoes and goat cheese on the surface of the puff pastry.

In a medium bowl, dissolve the cornstarch into 1/3 cup (75 ml) of the milk. Whisk the egg, the remaining 1/3 cup (75 ml) milk, the Parmigiano, the chives, and the salt and pepper into the cornstarch mixture.

Pour the liquid mixture over the tomatoes and cheese in the baking pan, or divide evenly among the ramekins.

Bake for about 25 minutes, or until between cheese is lightly browned.

Did you know that...

Milk is the primordial nutrient, maternal nourishment, pure white liquid par excellence. Not only is it a valuable food product in its natural state, it also lends itself to numerous modifications because of its capacity to take on a semi-solid or solid form through fermentation and curdling. Italians learned to manage the physical and biological transformation of milk, controlling and manipulating these changes with skill and originating an incredibly wide range of extraordinary cheeses: hard or soft, fresh or aged, blue, cow's milk, sheep's milk or goat's milk – the list of Italian cheese products is almost infinite. They can be considered fruits of the agro-pastoral Mediterranean cultures, but this didn't cause the wealthy and powerful to love them any less. Irrefutable evidence is provided by Pantaleone da Confienza's 15th century treatise, Summa Lacticinorum, *which was dedicated to these delicacies.*

Difficulty

FRIED STUFFED SQUASH BLOSSOMS

FIORI DI ZUCCA RIPIENI FRITTI

Preparation time: 40 minutes + 5 to 6 minutes cooking time

4 Servings

12 squash blossoms
6 oz. (180 g) zucchini (about
   1 medium), cut into thin strips
Salt and freshly ground black pepper
   to taste
3 tbsp. (40 ml) extra-virgin olive oil,
   plus more for frying
1 oz. (20 g) anchovies packed in oil
1 tbsp. (15 ml) warm water
1/3 cup plus 1 tbsp. (50 g) all-purpose
   flour

FOR THE FILLING
11 oz. (300 g) fresh ricotta cheese
2/3 cup (60 g) grated
   Parmigiano Reggiano cheese
6 fresh mint leaves, chopped
Salt and freshly ground black pepper
   to taste

FOR THE BATTER
3/4 cup plus 1 1/2 tbsp. (200 ml)
   cold water
1 2/3 cups (200 g) all-purpose flour
1 large egg

Difficulty

Method

Clean the squash blossoms and remove the pistils, being careful not to tear the petals.

Make the filling: Combine the ricotta, Parmigiano, and mint in a bowl, mixing with a wooden spoon. Season with salt and pepper.

Place the filling in a pastry bag. Gently pipe about 2 teaspoons of filling into each blossom. Gently twist the blossom to enclose the filling.

In a sauté pan, sauté the strips of zucchini with salt, pepper, and 1 tablespoon of oil until browned and tender.

Use an immersion blender to purée the anchovies, 2 tablespoons of oil (25 ml), and 1 tablespoon of warm water. Strain the anchovy dressing to remove any bone remnants.

Heat 1/2 inch (1 cm) of oil in a skillet until it is shimmering. Meanwhile, quickly whisk together the batter ingredients in a large bowl. Place the 1/3 cup plus 1 tablespoon flour in a separate bowl. Lightly flour the blossoms, dip them in the batter, and fry them in small batches.

With a slotted spoon, transfer the blossoms to paper towels to drain. Sprinkle with salt and transfer to individual serving plates. Serve the squash blossoms with the zucchini, drizzling the anchovy dressing over the top.

VEGETABLE CAPONATA
CAPONATA

Preparation time: 30 minutes + 15 minutes cooking time

4 Servings

1 lb. (500 g) **eggplant**
  (about 1 medium), diced
Salt and freshly ground black pepper
  to taste
1/2 oz. (15 g) **raisins**
  (about 1 1/2 tbsp.)
1/3 cup plus 1 1/2 tbsp. (100 ml)
  extra-virgin olive oil
2 oz. (50 g) **onion (about 1 small),**
  finely diced
2 oz. (50 g) **celery (about 2 small**
  stalks), finely diced
3 1/2 oz. (100 g) **zucchini**
  (about 1/2 medium), diced
1 oz. (20 g) **salt-packed capers,**
  rinsed and drained
2 tbsp. (15 g) **pine nuts**
1 oz. (25 g) **black olives**
3 1/2 oz. (100 g) **crushed**
  tomatoes (about 1 small)
1 tsp. (5 ml) **vinegar**
1 tbsp. (10 g) **sugar**
2 tbsp. (15 g) **pistachios**
1 **bunch basil leaves, torn**

Difficulty

Method

Put the diced eggplant in a colander, salt it lightly, and allow it to drain for about 30 minutes.

Soak the raisins in lukewarm water for 15 minutes. Squeeze them to remove excess water.

Heat 1/3 cup of the oil in a skillet over medium heat and fry the eggplant until tender, about 5 minutes. With a slotted spoon, transfer the eggplant to paper towels to drain.

Add the remaining oil to the skillet and heat over medium. Add the onion and celery and sauté until they begin to brown. Add the zucchini and sauté lightly. Add the raisins, capers, pine nuts, and black olives, stirring to combine. Add the crushed tomatoes and the fried eggplant. Season the mixture with salt and pepper; cook over low heat, stirring occasionally, for 3 minutes. Add the vinegar, sugar, pistachios, and basil; stir to combine.

To serve, spread the caponata on bruschetta or a sandwich, or offer as a side dish with fish or poultry.

SOUPS

CHAPTER TWO

CHICKPEA SOUP

MINESTRA DI CECI

Preparation time: 10 minutes + 12 hours soaking time + 1 hour 30 minutes cooking time

4 Servings

14 oz. (400 g) **dried chickpeas
   (about 2 cups)**
1 **bunch fresh sage**
3 1/2 tbsp. (50 ml) **extra-virgin
   olive oil**
3 1/2 oz. (100 g) **onions
   (about 1 1/2 small), sliced**
8 1/2 cups (2 l) **vegetable broth**
**Salt and freshly ground black pepper
   to taste**
1/3 cup plus 1 tbsp. (40 g) **grated
   Parmigiano Reggiano cheese**

Method

Soak the dried chickpeas in cold water overnight; drain.

Transfer the chickpeas to a pot with the sage, 3 tablespoons (40 ml) of the olive oil, and the onions. Mix well, add the broth, and cook over low heat for 1 1/2 hours. Season with salt and pepper.

For a creamier consistency, purée some of the chickpeas and add them back to the soup. Garnish the soup with the Parmigiano, sprinkle with the pepper, drizzle with the remaining olive oil, and serve.

Did you know that...

Like all legumes of Eurasian origin, chickpeas have been eaten for tens of thousands of years. The classical period was their golden age. They were already highly appreciated by the Greeks, and the Romans also ate them in many different ways. The poet Horace confirms that his contemporaries were very fond of a sort of "chickpea cake" that was sold by street vendors, who did very good business. But the ancient Romans also ate these legumes boiled or roasted, the way we often eat peanuts. But soup is definitely the dish that best represents chickpeas. Every region of Italy still has its own recipe for this substantial specialty (relatively simple, with one or more ingredients added), which has served as a daily meal for farmers over the last few centuries. Chickpea soup could probably be called the queen of traditional Italian popular dishes.

Difficulty

ROMAN EGG DROP SOUP
STRACCIATELLA ALLA ROMANA

Preparation time: 10 minutes + 1 to 2 minutes cooking time

4 Servings

4 **large eggs**
1/2 cup (50 g) **grated**
   Parmigiano Reggiano cheese,
   plus more for sprinkling
4 1/4 cups (1 l) **beef broth**
Salt to taste

Method

In a medium bowl, whisk together the eggs and the Parmigiano.

Bring the broth to a boil in a medium pot. Add one-third of the egg mixture, whisking constantly, to make shreds of eggs. Add the remaining eggs in 2 more batches, letting the soup return to a boil between additions. Once all of the eggs have been added, bring the soup to a final boil and use the whisk to break up any large clusters of eggs. Salt to taste. Serve the soup with additional grated cheese.

Did you know that...

Of all the Italian cheeses, Parmigiano Reggiano is without a doubt the most well known throughout the world, fully deserving the title of "king" of cheese products. The different types of Parmesan are still made using a technique that was refined over centuries, which calls for a perfect balance between man, animal and environment. Thanks to the monks who reclaimed the Po Valley and settled in the region, cattle breeding began on a large scale and allowed for large quantities of milk to be set aside for producing this aged, hard, "pasta cheese." To understand the extensive history of hard work and culture behind this extraordinary product, one need only consider that it takes 158.5 gallons (600 L) of milk to make a single wheel. Current scientific studies have only added to taste evaluations, demonstrating that this cheese has great dietary and nutritional value and confirming that it's a good choice for everyday consumption. In fact, Parmesan has been declared a healthy, safe, easily digested and nutritionally balanced product.

Difficulty

ITALIAN VEGETABLE SOUP
MINESTRONE

Preparation time: 20 minutes + 12 hours soaking time + 1 hour cooking time

4 Servings

3 1/2 oz. (100 g) **dried borlotti beans (cranberry beans)**
3 1/2 oz. (100 g) **dried cannellini beans**
8 1/2 cups (2 l) **water**
1/3 cup (80 ml) **extra-virgin olive oil**
3 oz. (90 g) **leek, white part only (about 1/2 medium), diced**
3 oz. (70 g) **celery (about 3 small stalks), diced**
7 oz. (200 g) **potatoes (about 1 1/2 medium), diced**
5 oz. (150 g) **zucchini (about 1/2 medium), diced**
3 oz. (80 g) **carrots (about 2 small), peeled and diced**
3 1/2 oz. (100 g) **pumpkin, peeled and diced**
3 1/2 oz. (100 g) **savoy cabbage, diced**
3 1/2 oz. (100 g) **green beans, diced**
Salt to taste
1 **bunch fresh parsley, chopped**
Parmigiano Reggiano cheese, grated, for garnish

Method

Soak the dried beans separately in cold water overnight; drain.

Place the beans in a pot of cold, unsalted water and bring to a boil. Lower the heat to a simmer and cook until the beans are almost tender, about 40 minutes; drain.

Meanwhile, bring the 8 1/2 cups (2 l) of water to a boil in a saucepan.

In a large skillet, heat half the olive oil over medium heat and sauté the vegetables for 4 to 5 minutes. Add the vegetables to the boiling water and bring back to a boil; then lower the heat and simmer for 50 minutes.

Add the cooked beans and continue to simmer for 10 minutes more. Season with salt and sprinkle with the parsley.

Garnish with the Parmigiano, drizzle with the remaining olive oil, and serve.

Difficulty

Did you know that...

Vegetable minestrone is prepared all over Italy, with many variations from region to region. The variety of vegetables can change according to personal tastes, but beans are the ingredients that should never be omitted.

CREAMY POTATO AND PUMPKIN SOUP WITH CANNELLINI BEANS
VELLUTATA DI ZUCCA E PATATE CON FAGIOLI CANNELLINI

Preparation time: 20 minutes + 12 hours soaking time + 45 minutes cooking time

4 Servings

7 oz. (200 g) **dried cannellini beans**
1 lb. (500 g) **pumpkin, peeled
 and chopped**
14 oz. (400 g) **potatoes (about
 3 small), peeled and chopped**
3 1/2 oz. (100 g) **onions
 (about 1 1/2 small), sliced**
6 1/3 cups (1 1/2 l) plus 8 1/2 cups
 (2 l) **water**
**Salt and freshly ground black pepper
 to taste**
1 sprig fresh **thyme, minced**
1 sprig fresh **rosemary, minced**
2 tsp. (10 ml) **extra-virgin olive oil**

Method

Soak the dried beans in cold water overnight; drain.

Place the pumpkin, potatoes, onions, and 6 1/3 cups (1 1/2 l) of water in a large pot and bring to a boil. Lower the heat to a simmer and cook until the vegetables are tender, about 20 minutes; then purée in a blender with their cooking liquid. Dilute with a bit of water, if necessary, and season with salt and pepper.

In another large pot, bring the remaining 8 1/2 cups (2 l) of water to a boil. Add the beans, lower the heat to a simmer, and cook the beans until they are tender, about 20 minutes. Stir the beans into the potato and pumpkin soup.

Garnish each serving with the thyme, rosemary, and pepper, drizzle with olive oil, and serve.

Did you know that...

Before other species arrived from America, the only beans known in Europe were of the dolichos variety, called fagioli dall'occhio *(eye beans) in Italian for the small black spot where the seed is attached to the pod. The "poor man's meat," as legumes were once known, always played a fundamental role on the tables of the lower classes. In fact, it's worth noting that unlike other products from the Americas, beans spread quite rapidly throughout Europe. People were already used to eating them (mainly in soups, mixed with grains) and it wasn't difficult to integrate them into the existing gastronomic and agricultural systems.*

Difficulty

LEGUME AND WHOLE-GRAIN SOUP

ZUPPA DI CEREALI E LEGUMI

Preparation time: 20 minutes + 12 hours soaking time + 1 hour cooking time

4 Servings

3 1/2 oz. (100 g) **pearl barley**
(about 1/2 cup)

3 1/2 oz. (100 g) **spelt** (about 1/2 cup)

3 1/2 oz. (100 g) **dried lentils**
(about 1/2 cup)

3 1/2 oz. (100 g) **dried Borlotti beans**
(cranberry beans) (about 1/2 cup)

5 oz. (150 g) **potato** (about 1 small),
peeled and diced

1/2 **clove garlic**

Fresh thyme to taste

6 1/3 cups (1 1/2 l) **water**

Salt and freshly ground black pepper
to taste

3 1/2 oz. (100 g) **frozen peas**
(about 3/4 cup)

1 tbsp. plus 2 tsp. (25 ml) **extra-virgin
olive oil**

Difficulty

Method

Soak the dried legumes and grains separately in cold water overnight; drain.

Place the beans in a large pot with the potato, garlic, thyme, and 6 1/3 cups (1 1/2 l) of water and bring to a boil. Add the grains and cook according to times on package instructions, about 20 minutes.

Toward the end of cooking, season the soup with salt, add the peas, and cook for about 3 more minutes. Garnish the soup with pepper, drizzle with the olive oil, and serve.

Did you know that...

Triticum dicoccum is a grain known as farro, which has been widely cultivated since antiquity and played a fundamental role in the alimentary history of classical civilization. In fact, the Romans actually made puls *(which can be translated as "polenta") from* farro. Puls *became a bona fide "national dish" for quite some time, especially during the austere and frugal period of the Roman Republic. It was eaten daily by the legionaries and the general population, and it was a staple food for the slaves. It was so widely used that the Italian term* farina *(flour) derived from the very grain that was used to make it. Farro was even at the center of an ancient Roman marriage ceremony called* confarreatio *(literally "the sharing of farro"). The bride and groom would eat a piece of farro cake (no point in lingering over the symbolic meaning of this) in the presence of the supreme pontiff and ten citizens who served as witnesses. The playwright Plautus (3rd-2nd century BC) made reference to the Greeks' habit of taunting the Romans by calling them* pultiphagi *(southern Italians still jokingly refer to their fellow citizens from the north as* polentoni, *which literally means "big polentas"), almost as if asserting their cultural superiority, even in a culinary context. Farro has now become something of a niche grain, but it has surely left an indelible mark on Italian cooking and eating habits.*

BROCCOLI PURÉE WITH CROUTONS AND WALNUTS

CREMA DI BROCCOLI CON PANE CROCCANTE E NOCI

Preparation time: 20 minutes + 45 minutes cooking time

4 Servings

1 lb. (500 g) broccoli, cut into florets,
  plus more florets for garnish,
  if desired
1 1/3 lbs. (600 g) potatoes
  (about 3 medium), peeled and diced
3 1/2 oz. (100 g) onions
  (about 1 1/2 small), sliced
6 1/3 cups (1 1/2 l) water
Salt and freshly ground black pepper
  to taste
2 oz. (60 g) day-old bread, diced
  (about 1 3/4 cups)
2 tsp. (10 ml) extra-virgin olive oil,
  plus more for baking sheet
4 walnuts, cut into pieces

Method

Put the vegetables in a saucepan with the 6 1/3 cups (1 1/2 l) of water and boil them, then purée them when they're done.

Dilute the purée with a bit of water if necessary and season with salt and pepper to taste.

Dice the bread and toast it in a nonstick pan with a bit of oil.

Garnish each serving with the croutons, a broccoli floret, and a few walnut pieces. Drizzle with olive oil and serve.

Did you know that...

In the past, food was often a sign of individual identity and social belonging, and in some ways it still is. During the Middle Ages, the ecclesiastical category clearly demonstrated a person's alterity in comparison to others (through clothing and lifestyle). A monk's choice to follow a spiritual path, mortifying his body and denying himself all sensual pleasures, was even manifested in food. And medical and scientific theories at the time held that certain foods could induce temptation and incite inappropriate behavior in men of the church. So vegetable soups, which were often made with vegetables grown in the monastery gardens by the monks themselves, became a fundamental meal in the cloistral life. While the powerful flaunted their social status through food (abundant, rare, and original), farmers and the general population were left to a poor and simple diet without any choice in the matter. And in the middle, as far away and different from one end as the other, were the men and women of the church who renounced food as a sign of devotion. In short, as food historian Massimo Montanari emphasized, "even hunger became a luxury item" in the Middle Ages.

Difficulty

DITALINI AND BEANS
PASTA E FAGIOLI

Preparation time: 20 minutes + 12 hours soaking time + 1 hour cooking time

4 Servings

7 oz. (200 g) **dried white beans**

7 oz. (200 g) **dried cannellini beans**

7 oz. (200 g) **dried borlotti beans**
(cranberry beans)

2 tbsp. (30 ml) **extra-virgin olive oil**

7 oz. (200 g) **onions (about 3 small),**
chopped

3 1/2 oz. (100 g) **carrots**
(about 2 small), peeled
and chopped

3 1/2 oz. (100 g) **celery**
(about 4 stalks), chopped

1 sprig fresh **thyme**

8 1/2 cups (2 l) **water**

Salt and freshly ground black pepper
to taste

5 oz. (150 g) **ditalini**
(or other small pasta)

Method

Soak all the beans separately in cold water overnight; drain.

Heat the oil in a large pot and sauté the vegetables over medium.

Add the beans, the thyme, and the 8 1/2 cups (2 l) of water and bring to a boil. Lower the heat to a simmer and cook until the beans are almost tender, about 40 minutes. Season with salt and pepper, add the ditalini, and cook for an additional 10 minutes.

Did you know that...

The Italian culinary tradition is rich in first courses with cereals and legumes that should certainly be reappraised, such as pasta with beans, pasta with chickpeas, pasta with broad beans, rice and lentils, and rice and peas. These are not only particularly tasty combinations but they are also dishes with significant nutritional value. Indeed, the combination of cereals and legumes brings together vegetable proteins with a particularly high and complete biological content like those provided by animal source foods such as meat, fish, eggs and dairy produce.
Proteins are the building blocks for muscles, bones, skin, cartilage and blood and are made up of amino acids. Eight of these amino acids are called "essential" from a dietary point of view, because our organism, even though it requires them, is not able to syn-thesize them in sufficient quantities and therefore they must be supplied by the food that we eat. Some proteins are considered complete because they contain all eight essential amino acids: phenylalanine, isoleucine, lysine, leucine, methionine, threonine, tryptophan and valine. Cereals lack lysine while legumes have no methionine but when eaten together they provide all the essential amino acids and are therefore a source of complete protein and an excellent substitute for animal protein.

Difficulty

TOMATO SOUP
ZUPPA DI POMODORO

Preparation time: 10 minutes + 35 to 45 minutes cooking time

4 Servings

1 lb. (500 g) **ripe tomatoes
(about 5 small)**
1/3 cup plus 1 1/2 tbsp. (100 ml)
  extra-virgin olive oil
7 oz. (200 g) **yellow onions
(about 3 small), chopped**
3 **cloves garlic**
1/2 tsp. **cayenne pepper**
1 cup (250 ml) **water**
**Salt and freshly ground black pepper
to taste**
1 **day-old baguette**
1 cup (20 g) **fresh basil leaves, torn**

Method

Prepare the tomatoes by making an X-shaped incision on the bottom of each tomato and blanching them in boiling water for 10 to 15 seconds. Immediately dip the tomatoes in ice water, then peel them, cut them into four sections, remove the seeds, and pass the pulp through a vegetable mill.

Heat 4 tablespoons (60 ml) of the oil in a skillet. Add the onions along with the whole peeled garlic cloves and the cayenne, and cook until softened and translucent. Pour in the tomato purée and the 1 cup (250 ml) water and simmer, covered, over low heat for 25 to 30 minutes. Season with salt and pepper.

Dice the baguette and toast in a nonstick pan (without any fat) until the bread is completely dried out. Add to the soup with the basil and continue cooking until the bread has softened and thickened the soup, 10 to 15 minutes. Remove the garlic cloves. Drizzle the soup with the remaining olive oil and serve.

Difficulty

PASTA & RICE

CHAPTER THREE

FETTUCCINE WITH ITALIAN SAUSAGE AND LEEKS

FETTUCCINE CON SALSICCIA E PORRI

Preparation time: 5 minutes + 15 minutes cooking time

4 Servings

Salt and freshly ground black pepper
  to taste
2 tbsp. plus 2 tsp. (40 ml) **extra-virgin
olive oil**
11 oz. (300 g) **pork sausage**
12 1/2 oz. (360 g) **leeks, white part
only (about 2 medium), trimmed,
rinsed well, and thinly sliced**
1/2 cup (100 ml) **white wine**
13 oz. (360 g) **fettuccine**
1 1/2 tbsp. (20 g) **unsalted butter,
softened at room temperature**
1 3/4 oz. (50 g) **Parmigiano Reggiano
cheese, grated (about 1/2 cup)**
2 tbsp. **fresh parsley, chopped**

Method

Bring a large pot of salted water to a boil.

Heat the oil in a large skillet over medium. Add the sausage and cook until browned, breaking up the large pieces with a wooden spoon. Add the leeks to the sausage. After a few minutes, add the white wine. Cook for 10 minutes, stirring occasionally, until the liquid is reduced. Season with salt and pepper; simmer and add a little water.

Cook the pasta in the boiling water until it is *al dente*; drain, reserving a little of the cooking water. Add the fettuccine to the sausage and leeks mixture, adding the cooking water to thin the sauce, if desired. Stir in the butter until melted. Sprinkle with the Parmigiano, garnish with the parsley, and serve.

Did you know that...

The leek is a close relative of the onion, but it has a more delicate flavor. Leeks are one of the few ingredients that were considered a fundamental source of nutrition during periods of famine in the Middle Ages. Leeks have been eaten since ancient times: Although we do not know the exact date when they were discovered, there is no doubt that they were already cultivated 4,000 years ago on the banks of the Nile, as illustrated in the hieroglyphics inside the pyramids. Even the workers who built the huge buildings ate, among other things, leeks and onions. From the Nile Valley, leeks spread all around the Mediterranean, becoming extremely popular in ancient Rome, where the Roman Emperor Nero was given the nickname "il porrofago" (or leek eater) for his habit of eating a lot of leeks to clear his voice.
According to an ancient legend, on the eve of a battle against the Saxons, Saint David advised the Welsh to wear leeks on their hats to distinguish them from their enemies. After a great victory, leeks became one of the symbols of the Welsh, who wear hats with leeks on Saint David's Day.

Difficulty

ORECCHIETTE WITH BROCCOLI, TOMATOES, AND ALMONDS
ORECCHIETTE CON BROCCOLI, POMODORINI, E MANDORLE

Preparation time: 20 minutes + 15 minutes cooking time

4 Servings

Salt and freshly ground black pepper
  to taste
12 oz. (350 g) **broccoli, cut into florets**
3/4 oz. (20 g) **salted anchovies**
2 tbsp. plus 1 tsp. (30 ml) **extra-virgin
  olive oil**
1 **clove garlic, crushed**
7 oz. (200 g) **cherry tomatoes
  (about 12)**
14 oz. (400 g) **orecchiette**
3 oz. (80 g) **Pecorino cheese, shaved**
1 oz. (30 g) **almonds, sliced
  (about 1/4 cup)**

Method

Bring a large pot of salted water to a boil.

In another pot of salted boiling water, blanch the broccoli florets for 3 minutes; drain well.

With a wooden spoon, break up the anchovies. Heat the 2 table-spoons (25 ml) of oil in a large skillet over medium heat and sauté the anchovies and garlic. Add the broccoli then the tomatoes and cook over low heat for 5 minutes. Season with salt and pepper and drizzle with the remaining 1 teaspoon oil.

Cook the pasta in the boiling water until it is *al dente*; drain. Add the orecchiette to the skillet with the sauce and stir to combine. Garnish with slivers of Pecorino and the almond slices and serve.

Did you know that...

This shape of pasta is typical of Apulia and Basilicata but orec-chiette seem to have Provençal origins. In the south of France since medieval times, rather thick discs of pasta were formed with a hollow in the center made with the thumb. They became widespread in Apulia and Basilicata with the name of orecchiette, because they resemble small ears. They were brought to these regions by the Angevins who ruled there in the 13th century. According to other scholars, however, this pasta originated in the Sannicandro area of Bari, during the period of Norman-Swabian domination, between the 12th and 13th centuries. But it could derive from some recipes of Jewish origin, like Haman's ears.

Difficulty

FUSILLI WITH SALMON AND CHERRY TOMATOES

FUSILLI CON SALMONE E POMODORINI

Preparation time: 20 minutes + 12 minutes cooking time

4 Servings

Salt and freshly ground black pepper
  to taste
2 tbsp. plus 1 tsp. (30 ml) **extra-virgin
  olive oil**
3 1/2 oz. (100 g) **onions (about
  1 1/2 small), roughly chopped**
1 lb. (450 g) **salmon fillets, skinned
  and cubed**
12 oz. (350 g) **cherry tomatoes
  (about 21), halved**
11 oz. (300 g) **fusilli or penne**

Method

Bring a large pot of salted water to a boil.

Heat the oil in a large skillet over low heat and sauté the onions for 2 minutes. Increase the heat to high, add the salmon, and cook for 2 minutes per side until browned. Season with salt and pepper. Add the tomatoes. Reduce the heat to medium and cook for an additional 5 minutes, adding water as needed to keep the fish moist. Season with salt and pepper.

Cook the pasta in the boiling water until it is *al dente*; drain. Add the fusilli to the skillet with the salmon mixture. Sauté the pasta with the sauce for 1 minute and serve.

Did you know that...

The history of tomatoes (Solanum lycopersicum) *is inextricably linked to Italian cooking. Though its American origins are well known, this plant of the solanacae family can be considered thoroughly Italian. It was introduced to Europe in the 16th century for its decorative value, and it was long believed to be poisonous. Mysterious stimulant and aphrodisiac powers were attributed to the plant, and the name it was given in many European countries alluded to this (it's still contained in the Italian word pomodoro, from pomo d'oro or "golden apple" and pomo d'amore, or "love apple"). For the same reason, small tomato plants were commonly given to women as a message of love in 17th century France. According to some historians, the term was actually mangling of pomo dei Mori, or "Moors' apple" and refers to the similar appearance of tomatoes and eggplants (also from the solanacae family), a vegetable often used in Arab dishes. Tomato cultivation spread throughout the Mediterranean and found its ideal terrain and climate in the area between Naples and Salerno. But it took a long time for tomatoes to be incorporated into culinary traditions.*

Difficulty

PENNE ALL'ARRABBIATA

PENNE ALL'ARRABBIATA

Preparation time: 30 minutes + 15 minutes cooking time

4 Servings

Salt to taste

2 tbsp. (30 ml) **extra-virgin olive oil**

2 **cloves garlic, sliced**

Red chile pepper, fresh or dried, to taste

1 1/3 lbs. (600 g) **tomatoes (about 6 small), peeled and diced**

11 oz. (300 g) **penne rigate or tortiglioni**

3/4 oz. (20 g) **fresh parsley, chopped, for garnish**

Method

Bring a large pot of salted water to a boil.

Heat the oil in a large skillet over medium heat. Sauté the garlic and chile to taste until golden brown. (If you're using a fresh hot pepper, seed and slice it; but if you are using a dried hot pepper, wear disposable gloves and crush it by hand, or use crushed red pepper flakes.) Add the tomatoes to the skillet. Season with salt and cook for 15 minutes, stirring occasionally.

Meanwhile, cook the pasta in the boiling water until it is *al dente*; drain. Toss the penne with the sauce, garnish with the parsley, and serve.

Did you know that...

It seems absurd, but Christopher Columbus left for India in search of pepper and came back from America with peperoncino *(red chili pepper). The Europeans' discovery of America was partially due to the need for a safer and faster way to obtain spices, which were a valuable and fundamental element of aristocratic meals throughout the entire continent. But what Columbus found was not India, and the small, spicy plant he brought back was not ordinary pepper. Still, the somewhat similar taste along with the ease of working with peperoncino (compared to the more "difficult" spice from which it takes its name) led to its rapid spread, first in Spain and Portugal, then in other European countries. Unlike other American products (tomatoes, bell peppers, and especially potatoes), the chili pepper took only a few decades to make its way into local gastronomic cultures. Perhaps because it acclimated so perfectly to the Mediterranean climate, or because it was a spice affordable to all, peperoncino has now become indispensable to the majority of southern Italian cuisine.*

Difficulty

ROSEMARY PENNE

PENNE SAPORITE AL ROSMARINO

Preparation time: 20 minutes + 11 minutes cooking time

4 Servings

Salt to taste
2 tbsp. (30 ml) **extra-virgin olive oil**
2 tbsp. (20 g) **butter**
2 **sprigs fresh rosemary**
1 oz. (30 g) **pine nuts (about 4 tbsp.)**
3 1/2 oz. (100 g) **onions
(about 1 1/2 small)**
1 **clove garlic**
3 1/2 tbsp. (50 ml) **dry white wine**
Crushed red pepper flakes to taste
12 oz. (350 g) **penne**
3/4 cup plus 1 tbsp. (80 g) **grated
Pecorino cheese**

Method

Bring a large pot of salted water to a boil. Meanwhile, in another large pot, heat the oil and butter over low. Mince the rosemary, pine nuts, onions, and garlic together. Add the rosemary mixture to the pot and cook until the onions are soft but not browned, about 5 minutes. Season the mixture with salt and add the wine.

Raise the heat to high and cook until the wine evaporates for about 10 minutes. Lower the heat, add a pinch of crushed red pepper flakes, and cook for an additional 10 minutes.

Cook the pasta in the boiling water until it is *al dente*; drain, reserving 2 to 3 tablespoons of pasta water for the sauce. Add the pasta to the rosemary mixture along with about 2 tablespoons of pasta water; cook for 1 minute and add the remaining tablespoon of pasta water if needed to loosen the sauce. Sprinkle the Pecorino over the top and serve.

Difficulty

Did you know that...

It's best to mince the rosemary, pine nuts, onions, and garlic with a knife. A food processor would break them down too much.

SPACCATELLE WITH VEGETABLE RAGOÛT
SPACCATELLE CON RAGÙ DI VERDURE

Preparation time: 40 minutes + 9 minutes cooking time

4 Servings

3 1/2 oz. (100 g) **eggplant**
(about 1/4 medium)

Salt to taste

3 1/2 oz. (100 g) **carrots**
(about 2 small)

2 oz. (50 g) **celery**
(about 2 small stalks)

5 oz. (150 g) **red bell pepper**
(about 1 small)

5 oz. (150 g) **yellow bell pepper**
(about 1 small)

5 oz. (150 g) **zucchini (about 1 small)**

1 1/4 oz. (35 g) **shallot**
(about 1 medium)

2 oz. (50 g) **leek, white part only**
(about 1/3 small)

3 1/2 tbsp. (50 ml) **extra-virgin
olive oil**

7 oz. (200 g) **tomatoes**
(about 2 small)

4 to 5 **fresh basil leaves,
coarsely chopped**

11 oz. (300 g) **spaccatelle or other
short tube pasta, such as tortiglioni**

Difficulty

Method

Dice the eggplant, then place it in a colander, salt lightly, and allow it to drain for about 30 minutes.

Meanwhile, dice the carrots, celery, bell peppers, and zucchini. Peel and dice the shallot. Slice the leek.

Heat the oil in a large skillet and sauté the leek with the celery and carrots. Add the eggplant, then the bell peppers, zucchini, and shallot. Season with salt to taste.

Prepare the tomatoes by making an X-shaped incision on the bottom of each tomato and blanching them in boiling water for 10 to 15 seconds. Immediately dip the tomatoes in ice water, then peel, seed, and dice them. Add them to the other vegetables to form a ragoût. Continue cooking for a few more minutes. Add the basil.

Bring a large pot of salted water to a boil. Cook the pasta in the boiling water until it is *al dente*; drain.

In a serving dish, pour the ragoût over the pasta, toss to coat, and serve.

RIGATONI WITH PARMIGIANO REGGIANO CREAM

RIGATONI CON CREMA DI PARMIGIANO

Preparation time: 20 minutes + 11 minutes cooking time

4 Servings

Salt and freshly ground black pepper
  to taste
1 1/4 cups (300 ml) **fresh cream**
4 1/4 oz. (120 g) **Parmigiano Reggiano
cheese, grated (about 1 1/4 cups)**
12 oz. (350 g) **rigatoni**
**Balsamic vinegar (preferably
  from Modena)**

Method

Bring a large pot of salted water to a boil.

In a large skillet, bring the cream to a simmer over medium-low heat and add the Parmigiano, stirring constantly for about 5 minutes until the mixture reaches the consistency of a thick cream. Season with salt and pepper. Keep warm over low heat.

Cook the pasta in the boiling water until it is *al dente*; drain. Add the rigatoni to the skillet with the Parmigiano Reggiano cream and stir until well combined.

Drizzle with a few drops of balsamic vinegar and serve.

Did you know that...

The traditional balsamic vinegar of Modena is a very ancient product, documented since at least the 11th century. The first record of this exquisite vinegar, which is still produced in the same areas of Emilia, comes from the monk Donizone, in a work he dedicated to Countess Matilde of Canossa. In the past, the term acetum referred to an array of acetic condiments derived from the fermentation of must or wine, which were very popular in an era when recipes called for a predominance of sweet or sour flavors. As is often the case, this delicacy seems to have been created by accident – its story probably began when a small quantity of cooked must was forgotten in the cellar.
The vinegar is aged for years in wooden barrels (juniper, chestnut, oak, mulberry), which imbue the liquid they contain with scents and fragrances – no other aromas are added. The word "balsamic" comes from balsamico (balm), which in turn stems from the dual nature of this valuable product – for centuries it was actually used for therapeutic purposes.

Difficulty

WHOLE WHEAT CELLENTANI WITH PEAR AND GORGONZOLA

CELLENTANI INTEGRALI CON PERE E GORGONZOLA

Preparation time: 30 minutes + 10 minutes cooking time

4 Servings

Salt and freshly ground black pepper
  to taste
1 1/2 tbsp. (20 ml) **extra-virgin
  olive oil**
2 **heads endive, sliced**
Juice of 1 orange
2 **pears, such as Bartlett**
Juice of 1 lemon
12 oz. (350 g) **whole wheat cellentani**
4 oz. (120 g) **Gorgonzola cheese, diced**

Method

Bring a large pot of salted water to a boil.

Heat the oil in a large skillet over medium-low heat. Cook the endives until browned, 3 to 4 minutes. Add the orange juice and cook the endives for about 3 minutes more. Remove the pot from the heat. Season with salt.

Peel and dice the pears and place them in a bowl. Sprinkle them with lemon juice so they won't discolor.

Cook the pasta in the boiling water until it is *al dente*; drain. Add the cellentani to the skillet with the endive mixture and cook for 2 minutes. Add the Gorgonzola and pears and cook for 1 minute more. Serve immediately.

Did you know that...

Gorgonzola is one of the best-known and best-loved Italian cheeses in the world. According to legend, it was invented here around the 12th century by a cheese-maker called Piermarco Bergamo, who happened to mix the curd from the night before with that of the morning. In this way, he obtained a mixture in which mold formed. This cheese, produced in Lombardy and Piedmont, is made with raw full-fat cow's milk. It has a straw yellow color with green marbling, due to the formation of selected molds. There are two versions: the "dolce" or soft creamy version (with cream added to the milk) with green veining that gives it a slight spiciness, and the "piccante" or spicy version with a more compact texture and more veins that give it a stronger and more aromatic flavor. For Gorgonzola Dolce, maturing takes at least two months, while for the Piccante type it takes from 90 to 110 days. Gorgonzola stravecchio (mature Gorgonzola) that has been matured over many months, with a semi-hard texture, is brown and has a very strong taste.

Difficulty

DITALINI RIGATI WITH ANCHOVIES AND SUN-DRIED TOMATOES
DITALINI RIGATI CON ACCIUGHE E POMODORI SECCHI

Preparation time: 25 minutes + 9 minutes cooking time

4 Servings

Salt to taste
1/3 cup (40 g) **fresh breadcrumbs**
12 oz. (350 g) **ditalini rigati**
3 1/2 tbsp. (50 ml) **extra-virgin olive oil**
3 oz. (80 g) **anchovy fillets packed in oil, chopped**
8 **sun-dried tomatoes packed in oil, chopped**
1/2 cup (100 ml) **white wine**
1/2 **clove garlic**
Crushed red pepper flakes to taste
1 tsp. **minced fresh parsley**

Method

Bring a large pot of salted water to a boil.

In a nonstick skillet, toast the breadcrumbs over medium heat.

Cook the pasta in the boiling water until it is *al dente*; drain.

Heat the olive oil in a large skillet and cook the anchovies on low heat until they dissolve, about 1 minute, using a wooden spoon to help break them up.

Add the sun-dried tomatoes to the anchovies and stir to combine. Pour in the white wine and add the garlic, whole. Stir until the wine evaporates.

Remove the garlic and add a pinch of crushed red pepper and minced parsley. Add the ditalini to the skillet, stir to combine, and cook for 1 minute more.

Top with breadcrumbs to taste and serve.

Difficulty

FARFALLE WITH RICOTTA AND BASIL

FARFALLE CON RICOTTA E BASILICO

Preparation time: 10 minutes + 10 minutes cooking time

4 Servings

Salt and freshly ground black pepper
  to taste
7 oz. (200 g) **fresh ricotta cheese**
1 1/2 tbsp. (20 ml) **extra-virgin
  olive oil**
15 **fresh basil leaves**
10 **unsalted almonds,
  shelled and peeled**
1/2 cup (50 g) **grated
  Parmigiano Reggiano cheese**
1/2 **clove garlic**
3 1/2 tbsp. (50 ml) **fresh cream**
12 oz. (350 g) **farfalle**

Method

Bring a large pot of salted water to a boil.

Press the ricotta through a sieve into a large bowl and add the olive oil in a slow, steady stream, whisking constantly, until it is creamy.

Place the basil in a food processor with the almonds, Parmigiano, garlic, cream, and a pinch of salt and pepper. Blend, using the pulse function, until the sauce is smooth. Gently fold it into the ricotta.

Cook the pasta in the boiling water until it is *al dente*; drain. Add the farfalle to the ricotta sauce, stir to combine, and serve immediately.

Difficulty

Did you know that...

Add an ice cube to the mixture in the food processor. This will prevent overheating and keep the basil from discoloring.

PUMPKIN RAVIOLI
CAPPELLACCI DI ZUCCA

Preparation time: 40 minutes + 5 minutes cooking time

4 Servings

FOR THE PASTA

11 oz. (300 g) **all-purpose flour
(scant 2 1/2 cups)**
3 **large eggs**

FOR THE FILLING

2 1/4 lbs. (1 kg) **yellow pumpkin**
7 oz. (200 g) **grated
Parmigiano Reggiano cheese,
plus more for sprinkling**
1 **large egg**
Salt to taste
Ground nutmeg

4 tbsp. **unsalted butter**

Method

Make the pasta: Place the flour on a clean work surface and make a well in the center. Add the eggs to the well. Gradually incorporate the eggs into the flour until you obtain a smooth dough. Wrap the dough in plastic wrap and refrigerate for at least 30 minutes.

Make the filling: Heat the oven to 350°F (175°C). Cut the pumpkin in half and scoop out the seeds and fibers. In a shallow baking dish filled halfway with water, place the pumpkin halves face down and cover with aluminum foil. Bake in the oven until the pumpkin is tender, about 1 1/2 hours.

Let the cooked pumpkin cool, then peel it, scoop out the flesh, and press it through a sieve into a large bowl. Add the Parmigiano and the egg and season with salt and nutmeg to taste. Let the filling rest for about 30 minutes.

Roll out the dough into 2 thin sheets. On one sheet spoon 1 to 2 teaspoons of the filling into mounds, leaving 1/2 to 3/4 inch (1 to 2 cm) between mounds. Lay the second sheet of dough on top, draping it gently over the mounds. Press gently around the mounds. Cut around the mounds to form individual rounds. Press the edges of the rounds together to seal in the filling.

Bring a large pot of salted water to a boil. Cook the ravioli until *al dente*.

Melt the butter and dress the ravioli with the melted butter and a sprinkling of Parmigiano. This pasta can also be served with a bolognese sauce.

Difficulty

POTATO GNOCCHI WITH TOMATO AND BASIL
GNOCCHI DI PATATE AL POMODORO E BASILICO

Preparation time: 1 hour 15 minutes + 4 to 5 minutes cooking time

4 Servings

FOR THE GNOCCHI

1 3/4 lbs. (800 g) **all-purpose potatoes (about 4 medium)**

1 1/2 cups (200 g) **all-purpose flour or Italian "00" flour, sifted**

1 **large egg**

Salt to taste

FOR THE TOMATO SAUCE

2 1/2 lbs. (1.2 kg) **ripe tomatoes (about 6 large)**

5 oz. (150 g) **onions (about 2 small), finely chopped**

1 **bunch fresh basil leaves, torn**

3 1/2 tbsp. (50 ml) **extra-virgin olive oil**

Salt to taste

1 1/4 tsp. (5 g) **sugar (optional)**

1/3 cup plus 1 tbsp. (40 g) **grated Parmigiano Reggiano cheese**

Method

Make the gnocchi: Place the potatoes in a pot of cold unsalted water and bring to a boil. Cook the potatoes until tender, about 20 minutes. Drain well. When cool enough to handle, peel the potatoes and put them through a food mill or mash them on a flat work surface.

Place the flour on a clean work surface and make a well in the center. Add the potatoes, egg, and a pinch of salt to the well and mix together, incorporating the flour until blended. Knead the dough briefly, then shape into logs about the width of a finger. Cut the logs into 1-inch (2.5 cm) lengths. If desired, shape the gnocchi by running them over the prongs of a fork while pressing slightly with your finger.

Make the tomato sauce: Prepare the tomatoes by making an X-shaped incision on the bottom of each tomato and blanching them in boiling water for 10 to 15 seconds. Immediately dip the tomatoes in ice water, then peel them, cut them in four sections, and remove the seeds.

Sauté the onions with 3 tablespoons (40 ml) of the oil. Add the tomatoes and half of the basil and cook for 15 to 20 minutes. Remove the basil and pass the sauce through a vegetable mill. Add the remaining olive oil. Season with salt. If the sauce is too acidic, add a pinch of sugar.

Bring a large pot of salted water to a boil and cook the gnocchi until they float to the surface. Remove with a slotted spoon. Serve them with the tomato sauce, topped with the remaining basil and the Parmigiano.

Difficulty

RICOTTA GNOCCHI WITH ARUGULA PESTO

GNOCCHI DI RICOTTA AL PESTO DI RUCOLA

Preparation time: 40 minutes + 2 minutes cooking time

4 Servings

FOR THE GNOCCHI

14 oz. (400 g) **fresh ricotta cheese**

1 cup (120 g) **all-purpose flour
or Italian "00" flour**

1 **large egg**

1/3 cup plus 1 tbsp. (40 g) **grated
Parmigiano Reggiano cheese**

**Salt and freshly ground black pepper
to taste**

Ground nutmeg to taste

FOR THE SAUCE

6 1/2 oz. (180 g) **ripe tomatoes
(about 1 large)**

4 oz. (120 g) **arugula**

5 tbsp. (70 ml) **extra-virgin
olive oil (preferably from Liguria),
plus more for drizzling**

Salt to taste

1/2 **clove garlic**

1/4 oz. (10 g) **whole shelled almonds,
plus chopped almonds for garnish**

2 tbsp. (25 g) **grated
Parmigiano Reggiano cheese**

Method

Make the gnocchi: Put the ricotta in a large bowl. Mix in the flour, egg, and Parmigiano until it forms a smooth dough. Season with salt, pepper, and nutmeg. Transfer the dough to a clean work surface and roll it out to 1/2 inch (1 cm) thick. Using a pastry wheel, cut the dough into small diamond shapes.

Make the tomato sauce: Prepare the tomatoes by making an X-shaped incision on the bottom of each tomato and blanching them in boiling water for 10 to 15 seconds. Immediately dip the tomatoes in ice water, then peel them, cut them into cubes, and remove the seeds.

Rinse and dry the arugula. Pulse it in a blender with the olive oil, a pinch of salt, the garlic, and the whole almonds. Add the Parmigiano, then the tomatoes, and pulse to blend.

Bring a large pot of salted water to a boil and cook the gnocchi until they are *al dente*; drain, reserving a few tablespoons of cooking water. Transfer the gnocchi to a bowl and toss with the arugula pesto, adding a bit of the cooking water and a drizzle of olive oil to adjust the thickness.

Garnish with chopped almonds, if desired.

Difficulty

RICCIOLI DI SFOGLIA WITH PROSCIUTTO, PEPPERS, AND PEAS

RICCIOLI DI SFOGLIA CON PROSCIUTTO, PEPERONI, E PISELLI

Preparation time: 15 minutes + 5 minutes cooking time

4 Servings

7 oz. (200 g) **red bell peppers
(about 1 1/2 medium)**
1 tbsp. (15 ml) **extra-virgin olive oil**
2 tbsp. (30 g) **unsalted butter**
5 oz. (150 g) **Parma ham, in one slice
about 1/8 inch (3 mm) thick, finely
diced**
3/4 cup plus 1 1/2 tbsp. (200 ml)
fresh cream
**Salt and freshly ground black pepper
to taste**
12 oz. (350 g) **garganelli
("riccioli di sfoglia")**
3 1/2 oz. (100 g) **peas (about 2/3 cup)**
2/3 cup (60 g) **grated
Parmigiano Reggiano cheese**

Method

To roast the peppers, heat the oven to 425°F (220°C) with a rack in the middle of the oven. Line a heavy-duty rimmed baking sheet with foil. Cut the peppers in half lengthwise and remove the stem, seeds, core, and ribs. Put the pepper halves on the baking sheet cut side down. Drizzle the oil over the peppers and rub it around to coat the skins evenly. Roast in the oven until the peppers are soft and slightly shriveled and browned, about 20 minutes. Let rest until cool enough to handle. Scrape away the pepper skin and cut the flesh into 1/2-inch (1 cm) dice.

Melt the butter over low heat and add the prosciutto. Cook until the prosciutto has browned. Add the roasted bell peppers. Cook for just a few seconds, then add the cream. Cook over low heat until the sauce reaches a boil. Remove it from the heat, season with salt and pepper, and keep it warm.

Bring a large pot of salted water to a boil and cook the pasta until 3 to 5 minutes before it is *al dente*, according to the package instructions. Add the peas to the gemelli and cook for the remaining time; drain.

Toss the pasta and peas with the sauce and stir in the grated Parmigiano. Serve immediately.

Did you know that...

A tasty alternative to prosciutto is sausage, cut into 1/3- to 3/4-inch (1 to 2 cm) pieces.

Difficulty

BAKED FARFALLE WITH VEGETABLES

FARFALLE GRATINATE DELL'ORTOLANO

Preparation time: 40 minutes + 15 to 20 minutes cooking time

4 Servings

FOR THE SAUCE

2 1/4 lbs. (1 kg) **eggplants**
  (about 2 medium)
Vegetable oil for frying, as needed
1 3/4 oz. (50 g) **carrot (about 1 small)**
1 3/4 oz. (50 g) **yellow or red bell**
  pepper (about 1/3 small)
3 1/2 oz. (100 g) **fresh tomato**
  (about 1 small)
3 1/2 oz. (100 g) **zucchini**
  (about 1/2 medium)
2 tbsp. (30 ml) **extra-virgin olive oil**
1 tsp. **fresh parsley, chopped**
Salt and freshly ground black pepper
  to taste
12 oz. (350 g) **farfalle**
5 oz. (150 g) **Caciocavallo**
  or Provolone cheese, diced
1/2 cup (150 g) **grated**
  Parmigiano Reggiano cheese

FOR THE BÉCHAMEL

1 1/2 oz. (40 g) **unsalted butter**
1/3 cup (40 g) **all-purpose flour**
2 cups (500 ml) **milk**
Salt and grated nutmeg to taste

Difficulty

Method

Make the sauce: Cut 1 eggplant into slices about 1/8 inch (3 mm) thick, using a mandoline. Place the slices in a colander, salt lightly, and let drain for about 30 minutes.

Heat at least 1/2 inch (1 cm) of vegetable oil in a skillet until shimmering. Fry the eggplant until tender. Transfer to a plate lined with paper towels to drain.

Dice the other eggplant, the carrot, bell pepper, tomato, and zucchini. In another large skillet, heat the olive oil over medium and sauté the vegetables. Add the parsley and season with salt and pepper.

Make the béchamel: Melt the butter in a heavy-bottomed pan. To make a roux, add the flour and whisk the butter and flour together for 3 to 4 minutes over low heat, until smooth.

Heat the milk in a separate pan, then add it to the roux, pouring it in a slow stream. Season with salt and nutmeg and continue cooking, whisking constantly, until the sauce is thick and creamy. If the béchamel is too thick, add a bit of milk. If it is too thin, let it cook for a few additional minutes.

Heat the oven to 365°F (185°C). Bring a pot of salted water to a boil and cook the farfalle until 1 to 2 minutes before the package instructions indicate for *al dente*. Mix the farfalle with the vegetables, the béchamel, and the Caciocavallo.

Line a 9 inch (23 cm) baking pan with the fried eggplant slices, arrange the pasta-and-vegetable mixture on top, and sprinkle with the grated Parmigiano.

Bake for 15 to 20 minutes, or until golden brown. Run a knife around the edge of the pan and invert the pan over a serving plate so that vegetable crust is on top.

CELLENTANI PASTA SALAD WITH TUNA AND PEPPERS

INSALATA DI CELLENTANI CON TONNO E PEPERONI

Preparation time: 45 minutes + 8 minutes cooking time

4 Servings

2/3 cup (150 ml) **extra-virgin olive oil,**
  plus more for drizzling

2 **sprigs fresh thyme**

11 oz. (300 g) **tuna fillet**

Salt and freshly ground black pepper
  to taste

12 oz. (350 g) **cellentani**

1/2 lb. (250 g) **red bell peppers**
  (about 2 medium)

1/2 lb. (250 g) **yellow bell peppers**
  (about 2 medium)

1 **clove garlic, thinly sliced**

1 1/2 oz. (40 g) **capers**
  (about 4 1/2 tbsp.)

1 tsp. **minced fresh parsley**

Method

Combine the 2/3 cup (150 ml) of olive oil and the thyme in a large bowl. Add the tuna and let it marinate for 15 minutes. Remove the thyme sprigs, remove the leaves, and set aside.

Bring a large pot of salted water to a boil. Meanwhile, heat a sauté pan over medium heat and cook the tuna, seasoning it lightly with salt and pepper, for about 1 minute per side. Let it cool and slice it against the grain into pieces about 1/8 inch (3 mm) thick.

Cook the pasta in the boiling water until it is barely *al dente*; drain the cellentani, rinse in cold water, and drain again. Transfer the pasta to a large bowl and drizzle with olive oil to keep it from sticking together.

Heat the oven to 350°F (175°C). Place the whole bell peppers on a foil-lined baking pan, drizzle them with olive oil, and rub them to coat. Roast in the oven until the peppers are soft and slightly shriveled and browned, about 20 minutes. Let cool. When they are cool enough to handle, peel and seed them, and cut them into medium dice.

Place the roasted peppers in a large bowl and add the garlic, the thyme leaves, and a drizzle of olive oil.

In a blender, purée the capers with 2 tablespoons (25 ml) of the olive oil.

In a large bowl combine the pasta with the peppers and the parsley. If necessary, add a bit of olive oil and a pinch of salt and pepper. Distribute the salad among serving plates and top each with a slice of tuna. Finish with a drizzle of caper oil.

Difficulty

DITALINI PASTA SALAD WITH GREEN APPLES, RAISINS, ALMONDS, AND SPECK HAM

INSALATA DI DITALINI CON MELA VERDE, UVETTA, MANDORLE, E SPECK

Preparation time: 20 minutes + 10 minutes cooking time

4 Servings

Salt and freshly ground black pepper
  to taste
12 oz. (350 g) **ditalini**
1/3 cup (80 ml) **extra-virgin olive oil,
  plus more for pasta**
2 **green apples**
Juice of 1 lemon
2 1/2 oz. (75 g) **raisins**
  (about 1/2 cup packed)
3 oz. (80 g) **speck ham**
3 1/2 oz. (100 g) **slivered almonds**

Method

Bring a large pot of salted water to a boil and cook the pasta until it is just *al dente*. Drain, rinse in cold water, and drain again. Transfer the ditalini to a large bowl and drizzle with a bit of olive oil to prevent it from sticking together.

Wash and core the apples, unpeeled. Cut them into 1/2-inch (1 cm) dice and place them in a bowl of cold water with half of the lemon juice.

In another bowl, soak the raisins in lukewarm water for about 10 minutes.

Meanwhile, cut the speck into 1/2-inch (1 cm) dice. Drizzle 1 tablespoon of the oil in a nonstick skillet over medium heat and sauté the speck until it is crispy.

Toast the almonds in a nonstick skillet for a few seconds. Drain the raisins, squeezing out any excess water. Drain the apples. Transfer the raisins and apples to paper towels to dry.

Whisk the remaining lemon juice with the remaining oil and a pinch of salt and pepper. Combine all the ingredients with the pasta, mixing well, and drizzle the lemon oil on top.

Difficulty

WHOLE WHEAT LASAGNE WITH WINTER VEGETABLES AND MONTASIO
LASAGNE INTEGRALI CON VERDURE E MONTASIO

Preparation time: 1 hour + 20 minutes cooking time

4 Servings

FOR THE PASTA

1 2/3 cups (200 g) all-purpose flour
  or Italian "00" flour
3/4 cup plus 1 1/2 tbsp. (100 g)
  whole wheat flour
3 large eggs

FOR THE FILLING

Salt and freshly ground black pepper
  to taste
3 1/2 oz. (100 g) chard (about 3 cups)
7 oz. (200 g) broccoli, cut into florets
1/4 cup (60 ml) extra-virgin olive oil
7 oz. (200 g) red onions
  (about 2 medium), julienned
7 oz. (200 g) pumpkin, diced
  (about 1 3/4 cups)
2 oz. (50 g) sun-dried tomatoes,
  chopped (about 1 cup)
5 oz. (150 g) white mushrooms, sliced
1 tsp. minced savory
14 oz. (400 g) Montasio cheese or
  Asiago cheese (about 4 cups), grated
1 cup (100 g) grated
  Parmigiano Reggiano cheese

FOR THE BÉCHAMEL

1 1/2 oz. (40 g) unsalted butter
1/3 cup (40 g) all-purpose flour
2 cups (500 ml) milk
Salt and freshly ground black pepper
  to taste

Method

Make the pasta: On a clean work surface, combine the flours and make a well in the center. Crack the eggs into the well and lightly beat with a fork. Gradually mix the ingredients together until a smooth, uniform dough forms. Form the dough into a ball, wrap it in lightly oiled plastic wrap, and let it rest for 30 minutes.

Using a pasta machine or a rolling pin, roll out the dough into a very thin sheet. Cut the sheet of dough into rectangles, about 4 by 8 inches (10 by 20 cm).

Bring a large pot of salted water to a boil. Cook the pasta until al dente; drain. Immediately place the pasta in a bowl of ice water to cool. Drain and place on a clean kitchen towel to dry.

Make the filling: Bring another large pot of salted water to a boil. Blanch the chard. Drain it and then immediately plunge it in a bowl of ice water to preserve its color. Blanch, drain, and cool the broccoli in the same manner. Roughly chop the chard.

Heat 1/8 cup (30 ml) of the oil in a large skillet over medium. Sauté the onions until softened. Raise the heat to medium high and sauté the pumpkin for 3 minutes. Add the broccoli and chard, and then the sun-dried tomatoes.

In a separate skillet, heat the remaining 1/8 cup (30 ml) of oil over medium. Sauté the mushrooms with the savory. Add them to the chard mixture and season with salt and pepper.

Heat the oven to 400°F (200°C).

Make the béchamel sauce: Melt the butter in a heavy-bottomed pan. To make a roux, add the flour and whisk the butter and flour together for 3 to 4 minutes over low heat, until smooth.

Heat the milk in a separate pan, then add it to the roux, pouring it in a slow stream. Season with salt and pepper, and continue cooking,

whisking constantly to avoid the formation of lumps, until the sauce is thick and creamy. If the béchamel is too thick, add a bit of milk. If it is too thin, let it cook for a few additional minutes.

Lightly oil a 9-inch (23 cm) square baking dish and alternate layers of pasta with layers of vegetables, about 3 tablespoons of béchamel, a sprinkling of Montasio, and a sprinkling of Parmigiano. Continue until all the ingredients have been used, finishing with a layer of béchamel and the cheeses.

Bake the lasagne for about 20 minutes, or until golden-brown. Let it cool for 5 minutes and serve.

Difficulty

SCHIAFFONI STUFFED WITH RICOTTA, ZUCCHINI, AND PROSCIUTTO

SCHIAFFONI RIPIENI DI RICOTTA, ZUCCHINI, E PROSCIUTTO

Preparation time: 50 minutes + 10 minutes cooking time

4 Servings

FOR THE PASTA

Salt and freshly ground black pepper
  to taste
7 oz. (200 g) **schiaffoni or rigatoni**
3 tbsp. (40 ml) **extra-virgin olive oil,**
  plus more for pasta
7 oz. (200 g) **zucchini**
  (about 1 medium), finely diced
14 oz. (400 g) **fresh ricotta cheese**
 3 1/2 oz. (100 g) **prosciutto,**
  finely diced
3/4 cup plus 2 1/2 tbsp. (90 g)
  grated Parmigiano Reggiano cheese
1 tbsp. (15 g) **unsalted butter,**
  plus more for baking dish

FOR THE BÉCHAMEL

2 1/2 tbsp. (35 g) **unsalted butter**
1/4 cup (30 g) **all-purpose flour**
  or Italian "00" flour
2 cups (500 ml) **milk**
Ground nutmeg to taste
Salt to taste

Method

Make the pasta: Bring a large pot of salted water to a boil. Cook the pasta until 2 minutes before the package instructions for *al dente*. Drain, rinse in cold water, and drain again. Mix with a bit of olive oil to prevent it from sticking together.

Heat the oven to 375°F (190°C). Heat the oil in a large skillet over high heat. Cook the zucchini until it is crisp-tender. Let it cool, then mix it with the ricotta, prosciutto, and two-thirds of the grated Parmigiano.

Make the béchamel sauce: Melt the butter in a heavy-bottomed pan. To make a roux, add the flour and whisk butter and flour together for 3 to 4 minutes over low heat, until smooth. Heat the milk in a separate pan, then add to the roux, pouring it in a slow stream. Season with salt and nutmeg and continue cooking, whisking constantly, until the sauce is thick and creamy. If the béchamel is too thick, add a bit of milk. If it is too thin, let it cook for a few additional minutes.

Use a pastry bag to pipe the filling into the schiaffoni. Grease a 9- by 13-inch (23 by 33 cm) baking dish and spread béchamel sauce over the bottom and sides. Fill it with pasta and pour the remaining béchamel on top. Sprinkle with the remaining Parmigiano and a few slivers of butter.

Bake for about 10 minutes, or until the surface is golden-brown.

Difficulty

LASAGNE BOLOGNESE
LASAGNE ALLA BOLOGNESE

Preparation time: 2 hours + 25 to 30 minutes cooking time

4 to 6 Servings

FOR THE SAUCE

2 tbsp. (30 ml) **extra-virgin olive oil**

1 oz. (30 g) **celery (about 1 stalk), chopped**

2 oz. (50 g) **onion (about 1 small), chopped**

1 3/4 oz. (50 g) **carrot (about 1 small), peeled and chopped**

1 **bay leaf**

4 oz. (120 g) **ground beef**

3 1/2 oz. (100 g) **ground pork**

3/4 oz. (20 g) **pancetta**

Salt and freshly ground black pepper to taste

1/3 cup (80 ml) **red wine**

2 oz. (60 g) **tomato paste**

2 cups (500 ml) **water**

FOR THE BÉCHAMEL

2 tbsp. (30 g) **unsalted butter**

2 tbsp. (25 g) **all-purpose flour**

2 cups (500 ml) **milk**

Grated nutmeg to taste

Salt to taste

8 **sheets oven-ready lasagna**

3/4 cup (80 g) **grated Parmigiano Reggiano cheese**

1 1/2 tbsp. (20 g) **unsalted butter, cut into pieces**

Difficulty

Method

Make the sauce: Heat the olive oil in a large skillet over medium. Sauté the celery, onion, and carrot. Add the bay leaf and continue to sauté until the vegetables are golden-brown. Add the ground beef, ground pork, and pancetta and cook over medium high until the meat begins to brown. Season with salt and pepper. Stir in the red wine and cook until it evaporates completely. Lower the heat and add the tomato paste. Add the water (or enough to cover the meat mixture) and cook slowly over low heat for at least 30 minutes. Discard the bay leaf.

Make the béchamel sauce: Melt the butter in a heavy-bottomed pan. To make a roux, add the flour and whisk the butter and flour together for 3 to 4 minutes over low heat, until smooth. Heat the milk in a separate pan, then add to the roux, pouring it in a slow stream. Season with salt and nutmeg and continue cooking, whisking constantly to avoid the formation of lumps, until the sauce is thick and creamy. If the béchamel is too thick, add a bit of milk. If it is too thin, let it cook for a few additional minutes.

Heat the oven to 350°F (175°C). Butter a 9- by 13-inch (23 by 33 cm) baking dish and arrange the first layer of lasagna lengthwise. Evenly spread a layer of sauce over it, followed by the béchamel and a handful of the grated Parmigiano. Continue to layer the lasagna, sauce, béchamel , and Parmigiano until you have used the rest of the ingredients. Finish with the béchamel, a generous dusting of cheese, and a few pieces of butter. Bake the lasagne for 25 to 30 minutes, or until golden-brown. Let it cool for 5 minutes and serve.

SPAGHETTI CARBONARA
SPAGHETTI ALLA CARBONARA

Preparation time: 10 minutes + 8 minutes cooking time

4 Servings

Salt and freshly ground black pepper
  to taste
4 large egg yolks
3 1/2 oz. (100 g) Pecorino
  Romano cheese, grated
  (about 1/3 cup plus 1 tbsp.)
5 oz. (150 g) guanciale (pork cheek)
  or bacon
12 oz. (350 g) spaghetti

Method

Bring a large pot of salted water to a boil.

Beat the egg yolks in a large bowl with a pinch of salt and a little Pecorino. Cut the guanciale or bacon into thin strips, about 1/8 inch (2 mm) thick, or into small dice. Sauté the guanciale in a large skillet over medium heat until browned.

Cook the pasta in the boiling water until it is *al dente*; drain, reserving some of the cooking water. Transfer the spaghetti to the skillet with the guanciale or bacon and toss together. Remove it from the heat and add the egg yolk mixture and a little cooking water and mix for about 30 seconds. Mix in the remaining Pecorino and a dash of pepper and serve immediately.

Difficulty

Did you know that...

*According to the most widely accepted theories, the name "carbonara" is linked to the presence of ground black pepper. In the traditional recipe, it blackens the pasta so that it appears to be covered by coal (*carbone*) dust.*

SPAGHETTI WITH CLAMS
SPAGHETTI ALLE VONGOLE

Preparation time: 20 minutes + 13 minutes cooking time

4 Servings

Salt and freshly ground black pepper
  to taste
2 1/4 lbs. (1 kg) clams
1/3 cup plus 1 1/2 tbsp. (100 ml)
  extra-virgin olive oil
1 clove garlic, chopped
12 oz. (350 g) spaghetti
1 tbsp. (4 g) fresh parsley, chopped

Method

Bring a large pot of salted water to a boil.

Scrub and rinse the clams thoroughly under running water. Place them in a large skillet with 1 tablespoon of the oil over medium heat. Cover and cook them until they open (2 to 3 minutes), discarding any clams that do not open. Remove the skillet from the heat and shell half of the clams. (Set aside the clams in shells.) Strain the cooking liquid through a sieve and pour it back into the skillet with the clams for the sauce. Set aside.

In another skillet, sauté the garlic in the remaining oil until golden-brown. Add the shelled clams and the sauce and cook until it comes to a boil. Add the clams in the shell.

Meanwhile, cook the pasta in the boiling water until it is *al dente*; drain, reserving some of the cooking water. Toss the spaghetti with the clams and sauce, adding cooking water as needed. Sprinkle generously with salt, pepper, and parsley.

Difficulty

RICOTTA AND SAGE TORTELLI

TORTELLI DI RICOTTA E SALVIA

Preparation time: 1 hour + 5 minutes cooking time

4 Servings

FOR THE FILLING

1 lb. (500 g) **fresh ricotta cheese**
1/2 cup plus 1 tbsp. (50 g) **grated Parmigiano Reggiano cheese**
1 **large egg**
1 tbsp. **chopped fresh parsley**
Ground nutmeg to taste
Salt to taste
Freshly ground white pepper to taste

FOR THE PASTA

3 1/4 cups (400 g) **all-purpose flour**
3 **large eggs**
3 1/2 tbsp. (50 ml) **dry white wine**
Salt to taste

FOR THE SAUCE

1 1/2 tbsp. (20 g) **unsalted butter**
8 **fresh sage leaves**
1/3 cup plus 1 1/2 tbsp. (100 ml) **fresh cream**
1/2 cup plus 1 tbsp. (50 g) **grated Parmigiano Reggiano cheese**

Method

Make the filling: Combine all the filling ingredients in a large bowl and mix thoroughly. Set aside.

Make the pasta: Place the flour on a clean surface and make a well in the center. Crack the eggs into the well and lightly beat with a fork. Add the wine and salt and gradually mix the ingredients together until the dough is smooth and uniform. Form the dough into a ball, wrap it in lightly oiled plastic, and let it rest for at least 10 minutes.

Make the sauce: Melt the butter with the sage in a large skillet over low heat until heated through. Add the cream and cook for 3 minutes.

Assemble and cook the tortelli: Bring a large pot of salted water to a boil.

Roll out the pasta into thin sheets and cut out 2-inch (5 cm) squares. Place a walnut-size amount of the filling in the center of each and close with another square, sealing the edges well to prevent them from opening during cooking.

Cook the tortelli in the boiling water until it floats; remove with a slotted spoon.

Toss the tortelli with the sauce over medium heat. Add the Parmigiano and serve immediately.

Difficulty

RISOTTO WITH ASPARAGUS

RISOTTO AGLI ASPARAGI

Preparation time: 15 minutes + 20 minutes cooking time

4 Servings

2 1/4 lbs. (1 kg) **asparagus**

Salt and freshly ground black pepper
  to taste

1 stick (120 g) **unsalted butter**

2 oz. (50 g) **onion (about 1 small),**
  chopped

1 lb. (500 g) **Arborio rice (2 1/2 cups)**

5 oz. (150 g) **Taleggio or similar**
  cheese (about 1 1/2 cups), grated

Method

Wash the asparagus and cut to equal lengths. Peel the fibrous ends.

Cut the tips off and set aside, then cut the stalks into 1/4-inch rounds.

Bring 6 cups (1 1/2 l) of salted water to a boil in a skillet. Cook the asparagus stalks until they are crisp-tender, about 10 minutes. Reserve the asparagus water for cooking the rice.

Melt 2 teaspoons (10 g) of the butter in a large skillet and sauté the onion until translucent. Add the rice and cook until toasted, stirring to coat with butter. Gradually add the cooking water from the asparagus, a little at a time, stirring frequently and adding more as it gets absorbed. Add the asparagus (stalks and tips). Remove from the heat and add the remaining butter, and the Taleggio. Season with salt and pepper, stir well, and serve.

Did you know that...

Rice consumption in Italy has taken an ambiguous path with many ups and downs. The Arabs introduced to Spain and Sicily, but the rest of the Italian peninsula continued to view it as a different kind of grain. It was used for therapeutic purposes and sold in spice shops along with other imported items. The first record of rice crops being planted in northern Italy (and less sporadic rice consumption) dates to the 15th century. But the spread of rice hit another detour: it was considered a food particularly suited to the poor, the farmers, and the lower classes in general. Consequently, for reasons that were more symbolic than nutritional or gustative, it was prevented from making its way to the tables of wealthier families. It was only with the invention of delicacies like risotto *(in the north) and* timballi *and* sartù *(in the south) that rice started to break free of its reputation as a "poor man's food" and earn a place in the Italian tradition of high gastronomy.*

Difficulty

RISOTTO WITH PORCINI MUSHROOMS
RISOTTO AI PORCINI

Preparation time: 20 minutes + 18 minutes cooking time

4 Servings

11 oz. (300 g) **porcini mushrooms**
1 1/2 tbsp. (20 ml) **extra-virgin olive oil**
1 **clove garlic**
Salt to taste
1 tbsp. (4 g) **chopped fresh parsley**
1/2 stick (60 g) **unsalted butter**
2 oz. (50 g) **onion (about 1 small), chopped**
1 1/2 cups (300 g) **Carnaroli rice**
6 1/3 cups (1 1/2 l) **beef broth**
3/4 cup plus 1 tbsp. (80 g) **grated Parmigiano Reggiano cheese**

Method

Clean the mushrooms thoroughly, removing the soil and wiping them with a damp cloth. Slice them thinly.

Heat the oil in a large skillet and brown the garlic. Remove the garlic, add the mushrooms (reserving some for garnish), and sauté until browned but still firm. Season with salt and parsley.

Melt 4 teaspoons (20 g) of the butter in a saucepan and sauté the onion until translucent. Add the rice and cook until toasted, stirring to coat with the butter. Gradually add the broth, 1/2 cup (250 ml) at a time, stirring frequently and adding more as it gets absorbed. Add the mushrooms and stir to combine. Continue cooking until all the broth has been absorbed and the rice is *al dente*. Remove it from the heat and mix in the remaining butter and the Parmigiano. Garnish with the reserved mushrooms and serve.

Did you know that...

The story goes that Roman emperor Claudius (10-54 AD) died of his own gluttony. His wicked and extremely ambitious wife, Agrippa, wanted her son by a previous marriage, Nero, to ascend to the throne. To speed things up, she decided to kill her husband by taking advantage of his well-known predilection for mushrooms. Like many of his contemporaries, Claudius was indeed a big fan of these exquisite and mysterious products of the soil. So his wife had some of the most poisonous boletes collected, cooked to perfection, and served. The emperor devoured them enthusiastically and met his famous end. Whether this is truth or legend, the fact remains that wild mushrooms – delicious, yet potentially poisonous or even lethal – have always held a dubious fascination for humans, and eating them safely requires great skill and knowledge, as much today as it did back then.

Difficulty

MILANESE-STYLE RISOTTO
RISOTTO ALLA MILANESE

Preparation time: 30 minutes + 20 minutes cooking time

4 Servings

5 1/2 tbsp. (80 g) **unsalted butter**

2 oz. (50 g) **onion (about 1 small), finely chopped**

1 1/2 cups (320 g) **Superfino rice or Arborio rice**

1/2 cup (100 ml) **white wine**

2 oz. (50 g) **beef bone marrow, crumbled**

4 1/4 cups (1 l) **beef broth, heated**

1 **pinch saffron powder (or one 0.125 g packet) plus 1/4 oz. saffron pistils**

Salt and freshly ground black pepper to taste

2/3 cup **grated Parmigiano Reggiano cheese**

Method

Melt half the butter in a large skillet and sauté the onion until translucent. Add the rice and cook until toasted, about 1 minute, stirring to coat with the butter. Add the white wine and cook, continuing to stir, until the wine evaporates, about 5 minutes; then add the beef bone marrow. Gradually add the broth, 1/2 cup (250 ml) at a time, stirring frequently and adding more as it gets absorbed. Add the saffron and season with salt and pepper.

Continue cooking until all of the broth has been absorbed and the rice is *al dente*. Remove it from the heat and mix in the remaining butter and the Parmigiano.

Difficulty

Did you know that...

This is the dish that symbolizes Lombardy. The simplicity of the rice is enhanced by the flavor and the color of saffron.

MAIN COURSES

CHAPTER FOUR

BEEF FILET WITH BALSAMIC VINEGAR

FILETTO DI MANZO ALL'ACETO BALSAMICO

Preparation time: 20 minutes + 25 minutes cooking time

4 Servings

1 3/4 lbs. (800 g) **beef filet**
Salt and freshly ground black pepper
  to taste
1 1/2 oz. (40 g) **all-purpose flour**
  (about 1/3 cup)
2 tbsp. (30 ml) **extra-virgin olive oil**
1/4 cup (60 ml) **balsamic vinegar**
1/2 cup (100 ml) **beef broth**

Method

Cut the filet into four 1- to 1 1/2-inch (2.5 to 4 cm) thick slices, depending on the width of the meat. Season with salt and pepper and dredge in flour, shaking off any excess.

Heat the oil in a large skillet over medium-high to high heat until it shimmers. Cook the filet for about 2 minutes per side, then remove the fat (but retain the juices). Add the balsamic vinegar and cook until the vinegar evaporates, 7 to 10 minutes.

Transfer the filet to a serving plate. Add the broth to the pan and cook over low heat, stirring constantly, until the sauce thickens, 10 to15 minutes. Pour the sauce over the filet and serve.

Did you know that...

In the Italian gastronomic tradition, as in many others, there are various established cooking methods that harbor symbolic meanings. Roasting is a perfect example of this. Technically a fire and a spit would suffice for roasting meat. In the Middle Ages, an era when even eating habits denoted social status, consuming roasted meat had a specific meaning. First and foremost, meat (especially red meat) was a luxury afforded to a privileged few. Secondly, the almost primitive simplicity of this cooking method made it ideal for the noble warrior classes, whose stomachs were as powerful as their swords. At the time, every class, genre, age, and type of human had its own diet, cemented over centuries, which was based on the standards of either Hippocratic or Aristotelian dietary "science." Roasting, which evoked the concepts of strength, simplicity, and wildness, was the technique best suited to great monarchs, princes, and warriors.

Difficulty

BEEF BRAISED IN BAROLO WINE

BRASATO AL BAROLO

Preparation time: 30 minutes + 12 hours marinating time + 3 hours cooking time

4 Servings

3 1/3 lbs. (1.5 kg) **beef shoulder**
1 **sprig fresh rosemary**
1 **bunch fresh sage**
1 **fresh bay leaf**
1 **clove**
1 **stick cinnamon**
3 to 4 **peppercorns**
2 **cloves garlic, chopped**
1 **onion, diced**
1 **large carrot, diced**
2 **stalks celery, diced**
1 **750-ml bottle Barolo wine
   (or any full-bodied red wine)**
3 1/2 tbsp. (50 ml) **extra-virgin
   olive oil**
Salt to taste

Difficulty

Method

Tie the beef shoulder with kitchen twine and put it in a bowl with the spices, herbs, and vegetables. Cover with the wine and marinate in the refrigerator for 12 hours. Remove the meat from the marinade and pat it dry. Strain the vegetables and reserve the marinade.

Heat the oil in a pot and brown the meat all over. Add the vegetables and continue to cook, then pour in the marinade liquid to cover, add salt, and cover the pan. Cook the beef over low heat for about 3 hours, until it is tender. When cooked, remove it from the pot and let it rest on a cutting board. Meanwhile, put the sauce through a vegetable mill (or blend in a food processor), strain through a sieve, and, if too thin, reduce to desired consistency. Cut the meat into thick slices and immerse in the sauce for 10 minutes before serving.

Did you know that...

It has a rich personality—refined and potent. Noble and generous. Barolo, produced in the Province of Cuneo, in Piedmont, is one of the finest Italian wines. It is obtained from the fermentation of three types of Nebbiolo grapes: Michet, Lampia, and Rosè. It has to mature for at least three years, two of them in oak or chestnut barrels. It takes its name from the Marquesses Falletti di Barolo, who were the first to produce it in the mid-19th century. They gave 325 carrà, *special oval barrels mounted on a horse-drawn cart, to King Charles Albert of Savoy, who had expressed the desire to taste the new wine that everyone was talking about. The sovereign was so enchanted by this wine—with a bouquet of rare complexity and smooth taste—that he decided to buy the estates of the Castle of Verduno, Pollenzo, and Santa Vittoria d'Alba to produce it. Barolo is the ideal accompaniment for all red meats, particularly game, but also for mature cheeses and dishes with truffles. It is excellent with roasts and in stews and braised-meat dishes.*

BEEF RIB-EYE STEAKS WITH ONIONS

COSTATA DI MANZO CON CIPOLLE

Preparation time: 15 minutes + 20 minutes cooking time

4 Servings

4 **well-aged rib-eye steaks**
2 1/2 tbsp. (20 g) **all-purpose flour**
2 tbsp. (30 g) **butter**
2 tbsp. (30 ml) **olive oil**
6 oz. (180 g) **onions (about 2 large), finely sliced**
1/2 cup (100 ml) **white wine**
Salt and freshly ground black pepper

Method

Lightly dredge the steaks in the flour. In a large skillet over low heat, melt the butter and add the oil. Add the onions and sauté until golden, 4 to 5 minutes.

Add the steaks, raise the heat to medium high, add the wine, and season to taste with salt and pepper.

When the steaks have browned nicely and to your liking, about 3 minutes per side for medium rare, serve them topped with the onions.

Difficulty

Did you know that...

Steak is such an ancient food that it is even pictured on the walls of the Etruscan tombs of Tarquinia. In Italy, costata, *or a rib steak, is one of the most common cuts for* bistecche *(steaks). In fact, the two terms have almost become synonymous.*

VAL PUSTERIA-STYLE GOULASH

GULASCH DELLA VAL PUSTERIA

Preparation time: 25 minutes + 2 hours 15 minutes cooking time

4 Servings

2 tbsp. (30 ml) **extra-virgin olive oil**
1 3/4 lbs. (800 g) **beef chuck,**
   cut into 2-inch (5 cm) pieces
5 **onions, chopped**
1 oz. (25 g) **all-purpose flour**
   (about 1/4 cup)
1 tsp. (5 g) **paprika**
3/4 cup plus 1 1/2 tbsp. (200 ml)
   red wine
1 **sprig fresh rosemary**
1 **fresh bay leaf**
1 **sprig fresh marjoram**
Zest of 1 lemon
1 oz. (30 g) **tomato paste**
Salt and freshly ground black pepper
   to taste

Method

Heat the oil in a large skillet over medium high and sauté the beef and onions for a few minutes until lightly browned.

Dissolve the flour and paprika in a little lukewarm water and pour over the meat. Add the red wine and simmer until it evaporates. Add the herbs, lemon zest, and tomato paste and mix well. Add at least a cup of water, cover, and simmer gently for at least 2 hours, until the meat is fork-tender. If it becomes too dry, add a little more water. Season with salt and pepper.

This dish can be served with polenta, boiled potatoes, or flour dumplings.

Did you know that...

Since the dawn of western civilization, the plant kingdom was part of the female domain. The gathering of fruits, flowers, herbs, roots, and berries, which were essential not only as part of the daily meal, but also for making therapeutic decoctions, infusions, and creams, was reserved for women. In this sense, women represented the intersection of popular medicine (which led the way to modern herbal science), cooking, and knowledge of the earth. Until a few decades ago, a wise old sage called the medicina was a common presence in the Italian countryside. Based on secret knowledge passed down from generation to generation, she cured common illnesses using natural remedies along with a few magical formulas.

Difficulty

BRAISED VEAL

VITELLO IN FRICANDÒ

Preparation time: 20 minutes + 1 hour 10 minutes cooking time

4 Servings

4 slices Parma ham, chopped
1 1/3 lbs. (600 g) **veal flank**
4 whole cloves
5 oz. (150 g) **onions (about 2 small)**,
  peeled
3 1/2 tbsp. (50 g) **unsalted butter**
1 carrot, diced small
1 bunch fresh parsley
4 celery leaves
3 1/2 tbsp. (50 ml) **dry white wine**
Salt and freshly ground black pepper
  to taste
Beef broth, as needed

Method

Remove the fat from the ham and use it to lard the veal.

Stick the cloves into the whole onions. Heat the butter in a large skillet over high heat and fry the ham and the onions. Fry the mixture well, then add the veal and brown it all over.

Add the carrot. Make a bundle of the parsley and celery leaves and add it to the pan. Add the white wine, season with salt and pepper, and cover. Cook the veal over low heat, turning it frequently.

If, during cooking, the meat becomes too dry, add a little broth. Cook until the meat is fork-tender, about 1 hour. Strain the vegetables from the juices (reserving the juices). Cut the veal into thin slices. Pour some of the juices over the veal and serve with the vegetables alongside.

Difficulty

VEAL BOCCONCINI WITH POTATOES AND PEAS
BOCCONCINI DI VITELLO CON PATATE E PISELLI

Preparation time: 20 minutes + 1 hour 15 minutes cooking time

4 Servings

1 1/2 tbsp. (20 g) **unsalted butter**
3 1/2 tbsp. (50 ml) **extra-virgin olive oil**
1 oz. (25 g) **leek, white and pale green parts only (about 1 small), sliced**
3 1/2 oz. (100 g) **onions (about 1 1/2 small), chopped**
1/3 cup (30 g) **celery (about 1 stalk), chopped**
1 1/3 lbs. (600 g) **veal, cut into bite-size pieces**
Salt and freshly ground black pepper to taste
1/2 cup (100 ml) **white wine**
4 cups (1 l) **vegetable or beef broth**
7 oz. (200 g) **potatoes (about 1 1/2 medium), peeled and cut into sticks**
1/2 cup plus 3 tbsp. (100 g) **peas**
1/3 cup plus 1 1/2 tbsp. (100 ml) **milk**

Method

Heat the butter and oil in a skillet over medium and sauté the leek, onions, and celery. Add the veal and brown all together.

Season with salt and pepper and add the white wine and cook until the wine evaporates. Gradually add the broth and continue to cook for about 1 hour.

Blanch the potatoes for 5 minutes in boiling salted water, drain, and add to the veal mixture. Add the peas and continue cooking for about 15 minutes.

Lastly, add the milk and reduce the sauce to a desired consistency. Serve.

Difficulty

Did you know that...

Potatoes, like other Solanaceae, contain several toxins, particularly an alkaloid called solanine, so they should never be cooked when they have parts that are green or have started sprouting. It is best to store them in the dark and eat them without the skins, because it is there that the majority of the solanine, is concentrated and is not eliminated with cooking.

MILANESE-STYLE OSSO BUCO

OSSIBUCHI ALLA MILANESE

Preparation time: 20 minutes + 1 hour 40 minutes cooking time

4 Servings

4 bone-in veal shanks, of about
  14 oz. (300 to 400 g) each
Salt and freshly ground black pepper
  to taste
1 3/4 oz. (100 g) **all-purpose flour
  (about 3/4 cup)**
3 1/2 oz. (100 g) **unsalted butter**
3 1/2 oz. (100 g) **onions
  (about 1 1/2 small), thinly sliced**
1/2 cup (100 ml) **dry white wine**
1 cup (250 ml) **beef broth**
1 **clove garlic, finely chopped**
1 **bunch fresh parsley, finely chopped**
1 **sprig fresh rosemary, finely chopped**
Zest of 1/2 lemon

Difficulty

Method

Season the veal shanks with salt and pepper and dredge them in the flour, shaking off any excess.

In a large skillet, melt the butter over medium high and brown the veal on both sides. Remove from the skillet and set aside.

Add the onions to the skillet and sauté over low heat until softened. Return the veal to the pan, add the white wine, and cook until it evaporates. Add the broth, cover, and simmer gently until the meat is fork-tender, about 1 1/2 hours.

Meanwhile, mix the garlic, parsley, rosemary, and lemon zest together in a small bowl. Sprinkle the herbs over the osso buco just before serving.

Did you know that...

Since antiquity, vegetable gardens have played a fundamental role in Mediterranean cuisine, so much so that even today almost every Italian country house has its own garden. The vegetable garden first acquired some prestige in conjunction with the monastic culture of the High Middle Ages. Various authors refer to them as a prefiguration of heaven on earth. The Italian landscape is decorated with vegetable gardens, their colors, and their borders (large or small). But what did the earth have to offer to the medieval table? Reading the Capitulare de villis *from the Carolingian era, Strabo's* Hortulus, *and Hildegard of Bingen's botanical treatise, the first thing we discover is that gardens at the time contained ornamental (some edible), medicinal, and alimentary plants. The latter includes cucumbers, melon, pumpkin, chard, spinach, onions, leeks, radishes, peas, and above all – cabbage, the undisputed king of the poor and humble kitchen. Herbs were also widely cultivated throughout the Italian peninsula, and their unmistakable fragrances helped to distinguish Italian cuisine from the rest of European cuisine.*

ROMAN-STYLE VEAL MEDALLIONS

SALTIMBOCCA ALLA ROMANA

Preparation time: 10 minutes + 10 minutes cooking time

4 Servings

8 veal top round slices, about
  2 to 2 1/2 oz. (60 to 70 g) each
8 slices Parma ham
8 fresh sage leaves
1/3 cup plus 1 tbsp. (50 g) **all-purpose**
flour
3 1/2 tbsp. (50 g) **unsalted butter**
Salt and freshly ground black pepper
  to taste
2/3 cup (150 ml) **dry white wine**

Method

Trim the slices of veal carefully and pound them gently with a meat mallet until they are 1/4 inch (1/2 cm) thick.

Place a slice of Parma ham and a sage leaf on top of each slice of meat. Flour the meat on the side without the ham. Secure with a toothpick (one variation to the traditional recipe is to roll up the saltimbocca).

Melt the butter in a large skillet until it turns frothy. Add the meat, ham side down. Sauté the meat, season it with salt and pepper, and turn it over for a couple of minutes. Remove the fat from the skillet and deglaze with the wine. Simmer until the wine evaporates and, if necessary, dilute the sauce with a few tablespoons of hot water. Serve immediately.

Did you know that...

Saltimbocca alla romana, a main course that is typical of the cuisine of Latium, is a dish that's known all over the world. It has been suggested that it may have more northern origins, with links to the city of Brescia in Lombardy; but Pellegrino Artusi, in his famous La scienza in cucina e l'arte di mangiar bene *(1891) (The Art of Cooking and Eating Well) writes about enjoying this delicacy in a historic Roman trattoria. In Italy, saltimbocca alla sorrentina is also appreciated. In this recipe, the slices of veal are briefly sautéed in a skillet, seasoned with salt and pepper, and then placed in a greased baking pan. The veal slices are covered with slices of mozzarella and Parma ham (or salami). They are then covered with tomato sauce flavored with oregano and parsley, sprinkled with a handful of Parmigiano Reggiano, splashed with a little white wine, and then cooked in the oven for a few minutes.*

Difficulty

VEAL STEW WITH POTATOES
SPEZZATINO DI VITELLO CON PATATE

Preparation time: 20 minutes + 45 to 50 minutes cooking time

4 Servings

3 1/2 tbsp. (50 g) **unsalted butter**

2 tbsp. (30 ml) **extra-virgin olive oil**

1 **carrot, thinly sliced**

1 **onion, thinly sliced**

1/2 cup plus 2 tsp. (60 g) **all-purpose flour**

1 3/4 lbs. (800 g) **lean veal, cubed**

1/2 cup (100 ml) **white wine**

2 3/4 oz. (80 g) **tomato sauce**

Salt and freshly ground black pepper to taste

4 **potatoes, cut into bite-size pieces**

Method

Heat the butter and olive oil in a large pot over medium. Sauté the carrot and onion until soft.

Lightly flour the veal, add it to the pot, and cook for a few minutes. Add the white wine, tomato sauce (which you can dilute with a little water, if you wish), salt, and pepper. When the liquid has reduced by half, add the potatoes. Cover with water and simmer, uncovered, for 45 to 50 minutes, until the meat and potatoes are tender.

Did you know that...

When you cook meat on the grill, you're repeating actions that often had a sacred air in classical civilization. In ancient Greece – as historian and anthropologist Marcel Detienne demonstrated – religious sacrifice often coincided with slaughter and the shared consumption of meat roasted over a fire. The priest in charge of this ritual was called the magheiros *(a name etymylogically linked to the Italian* macellaio, *meaning "butcher") and it was his job to slaughter the animal, divide it into pieces (strictly delineated by tradition), preside over the cooking, and finally, distribute portions to the people so the communal meal could begin. This act had an extremely high cathartic value according to beliefs of the time. The blood spilled on the altar and the purifying fire kept all types of contamination and other threats away from the community participating in the ritual. According to some historians, given the underdeveloped nature of the Greek economy and manufacturing practices, sacrifices were one of the few opportunities for citizens to eat meat. And the rhythm of this pagan rite is reproduced at every summer barbecue, in the gestures made and the practice of sharing food.*

Difficulty

MILANESE-STYLE CUTLETS

COSTOLETTE ALLA MILANESE

Preparation time: 20 minutes + 8 minutes cooking time

4 Servings

4 veal cutlets, of about 7 oz. (200 g)
    each, or 4 bone-in veal chops
All-purpose flour, as needed
2 large eggs
3 oz. (100 g) dried breadcrumbs
    (about 1 cup)
5 1/2 tbsp. (80 g) unsalted butter
Salt to taste
1 lemon (optional)

Method

Remove the excess fat from the cutlets or chops, if necessary, and then tenderize the meat with a meat mallet, pounding each cutlet to a thickness of about 1/4 inch (5 mm).

Dredge the cutlets or chops in flour, then dip them in egg, and, lastly, cover them with breadcrumbs, pressing lightly with your hands to make sure the breadcrumbs stick to both sides.

Heat the butter in a skillet over medium until frothy. Add the veal and cook for 3 to 4 minutes on each side, taking care to keep the butter from darkening or starting to smoke. Transfer the cutlets to paper towels to drain, salt lightly, and serve with a slice of lemon, if you wish.

Did you know that...

Along with risotto alla milanese *and* panettone, *cutlets are one of the most typical Milanese dishes. They're also at the center of an academic debate: Austria claims that cutlets are an Austrian dish. To date, however, there is no clear evidence to confirm if it was the Milanese-style cutlet that influenced the* Wiener Schnitzel *or if it was the latter that migrated to create an Italian variation. Milanese cutlets can be of two types: on the bone or the so-called elephant's ear type. In the former, the cutlet retains its original form and should be tenderized very slightly, if at all. It is about 1 inch (3 cm) thick and when cooked, it is still soft and slightly pink inside. In the latter case, the bone is removed and the cutlet is tenderized until it is a wide, thin slice that curls up at the edges as it cooks. It is a crispier version in which the flavor of the fried breadcrumbs dominates that of the meat.*

Difficulty

ROAST SHANK OF PORK
STINCO DI MAIALE AL FORNO

Preparation time: 30 minutes + 1 hour 30 minutes cooking time

4 Servings

4 pork shanks, of about 1 1/2 lbs. (700 g) each
Salt and freshly ground black pepper to taste
3 1/2 oz. (100 g) lard
3 1/2 tbsp. (50 ml) extra-virgin olive oil
1 onion, halved
2 cloves garlic
1 sprig fresh rosemary
1 cup (200 ml) dry white wine
4 1/4 cups (1 l) beef broth or water, plus more as needed

Method

Heat the oven to 400°F (200°C).

Arrange the pork shanks in a roasting pan and season with salt and pepper. Add the lard, oil, onion, the whole cloves of garlic, and the rosemary. Turn the shanks to coat them well in fat. Brown them over medium-high heat. Add the wine and cook over low until it evaporates.

Add the broth or water, cover the roasting pan, and place it in the oven. Continue cooking, turning the pork every 30 minutes and adding more broth or water if the meat begins to dry out. Roast until the pork is tender, about 1 1/2 hours in the oven.

Did you know that...

This is a method of cooking with slow constant heat that causes the meat to form a crisp golden crust on the outside while retaining the juices inside and, as a result, retaining its flavor. Roasted food is also very easy to digest because of the long cooking time. Roasting can be done in the oven, directly over a fire, on a spit, or in a saucepan but it is always done in two stages. The initial stage is frying, which is done at a high temperature to enable a superficial crust to form. In the second phase, the temperature is lowered so the heat reaches the center of the meat.
Traditionally, roasted meats include beef, veal, pork, chicken, turkey and game. Lean meat should always be barded with slices of lardo, bacon or fat ham to ensure that it remains soft, while white meat should be cooked a little longer than red meat, which should be left slightly rare. It is also possible to roast fish, above all those of medium to large size. They should be cooked whole so the skin protects the flesh from drying too much because of the heat. As far as vegetables are concerned, potatoes, peppers and eggplants are perfect for roasting.

Difficulty

TUSCAN-STYLE ROAST LOIN OF PORK

ARISTA ALLA TOSCANA

Preparation time: 30 minutes + 1 hour cooking time

4 Servings

2 1/4 lbs. (1 kg) **bone-in pork loin roast**
2 **cloves garlic, chopped**
2 **sprigs fresh rosemary, chopped**
Salt and freshly ground black pepper
  to taste
1/3 cup plus 1 1/2 tbsp. (100 ml)
  extra-virgin olive oil

Method

Heat the oven to 350°F (175°C). Partially separate the bones from the joint of meat without removing the bone.

Mix together the garlic, rosemary, a generous pinch of salt, and a pinch of pepper. Distribute half of the mixture between the bone and the meat. Tie the two parts of the joint together with kitchen twine. Distribute the rest of the garlic mixture over the outside of the meat, massaging well.

Place the meat in a roasting pan. Drizzle with the oil and roast in the oven for about 1 hour, or until a meat thermometer inserted into the center of the pork reads 155°F (68°C). Let rest for 10 minutes, remove the twine and the bone, and slice the meat. Serve with the warm cooking juices.

Did you know that...

According to legend, also told by Pellegrino Artusi in his La scienza in cucina e l'arte di mangiar bene *(1891), the name* arista *means loin of pork with the sirloin attached to the bone—a cut of meat that is often used in Tuscany for roasts, flavored with garlic, rosemary, and pepper. The name originated in Florence in 1439 when the Ecumenical Council of the Greek Orthodox Church and the Roman Catholic Church convened, organized by Cosimo the Elder. During one of the banquets, Cardinal Basilio Bessarione exclaimed the following of the excellent roast loin of pork: "Aristos, aristos!" meaning in Greek "The best, the best!" The Florentines present at the lunch liked this name and decided to use it for this cut of meat. However, there is a Florentine document dating back to 1287 that makes a reference to an "arista di porcho," and Franco Sacchetti writes about "un'arista al forno" in his novel written at the end of the 14th century. Arista can be eaten roasted, but it can also be eaten cold, especially in summer: It is sliced very thin and accompanied by a sauce made with extra-virgin olive oil and lemon.*

Difficulty

PORK AND CABBAGE STEW
CASSOEULA

Preparation time: 20 minutes + 3 hours cooking time

4 Servings

2 lbs. (900 g) **pork spareribs**
1 3/4 lbs. (800 g) **pork sausage**
7 oz. (200 g) **onions (about 3 small),** sliced
3 1/2 tbsp. (50 ml) **extra-virgin olive oil**
1 3/4 lbs. (800 g) **savoy cabbage, sliced**
1 2/3 cups (400 g) **crushed tomatoes (about 4 small)**
Salt and freshly ground black pepper to taste
Chopped fresh sage and rosemary to taste

Method

Place the pork spare ribs and the sausages in separate large pans of cold water. Bring to a boil, then parboil the meats for 10 minutes.

Meanwhile, sauté the onions in a large skillet with the olive oil. Add the cabbage and cook for a few minutes.

Add the crushed tomatoes, season with salt and pepper, and then add the meat. Cook over low heat for about 2 hours, until the meat is cooked through. Add the herbs and serve.

Did you know that...

This dish, eaten most often in the winter months, is typical of the cuisine of Lombardy and of Milanese cuisine in particular. The name cassoeula *probably derives from a dialect term meaning the spoon you use to mix the contents of the* casseou *or saucepan, i.e., the* casseruola, *in which it is cooked.*

This popular main course originated at the beginning of the last century, perhaps as a variation of the "peasant" dish traditionally prepared on the occasion of the Feast of St. Anthony the Abbot on January 17, which marked the end of the annual slaughtering of pigs. The cuts of pork used for cassoeula were the less noble parts, like the head, ears, rind, hocks, and spare ribs—they helped to add more flavor to this humble cabbage stew.

According to some historians, the cassoeula *eaten today is the simplified and poorer version of an opulent Christmas dish in which various types of particularly fatty and tasty meats were served around the cabbage and pork base. Even today, in some parts of northern Italy, like the Novara area, cassoeula is prepared with the addition of goose meat.*

Difficulty

PORK TENDERLOIN IN MARSALA WINE

FILETTO DI MAIALE AL MARSALA

Preparation time: 30 minutes + 15 minutes cooking time

4 Servings

3 1/2 oz. (100 g) **caul fat**

1 3/4 oz. (50 g) **lardo or bacon fat, finely chopped**

Chopped fresh sage to taste

Chopped fresh rosemary to taste

Chopped fresh thyme to taste

1/2 **clove garlic, finely chopped**

17 oz. (500 g) **pork tenderloin**

Salt and freshly ground black pepper to taste

1 3/4 oz. (50 g) **Parma ham, sliced**

All-purpose flour, as needed

2 1/4 tbsp. (30 ml) **extra-virgin olive oil**

3 1/2 tbsp. (50 g) **unsalted butter**

1/2 cup (100 ml) **Marsala wine**

Method

Heat the oven to 400°F (200°C).

Rinse the caul fat under running water.

Prepare a mixture of lardo or bacon fat and sage, rosemary, thyme, and garlic.

Trim any excess fat from the pork tenderloin, season with salt and pepper, and spread the lardo–herb mixture over it. Wrap it in the Parma ham and then in the caul fat.

Dredge the pork lightly in the flour and sauté in a large skillet with the oil and butter over medium heat, then add the bits of meat that you have trimmed off. Place in a roasting pan and roast in the oven for 12 to 13 minutes, or until a meat thermometer inserted into the center of the pork reads 155°F (68°C).

Remove the pork from the roasting pan and keep warm. Remove the excess fat, deglaze the baking pan with Marsala wine, and reduce the cooking juices as much as necessary. Slice the meat and serve with the sauce.

Difficulty

ROASTED TURKEY BREAST WITH HAZELNUTS
PETTO DI TACCHINO ARROSTO ALLE NOCCIOLE

Preparation time: 20 minutes + 1 hour 15 minutes cooking time

4 Servings

1 3/4 lbs. (800 g) **boneless turkey breast**

1/3 cup (80 ml) **extra-virgin olive oil**

Salt and freshly ground black pepper to taste

3 1/2 oz. (100 g) **onions (about 1 1/2 small), diced**

2 3/4 oz. (80 g) **carrots (about 1 1/2 small), diced**

2 oz. (60 g) **celery (about 2 stalks), diced**

2 **cloves garlic**

Fresh sage to taste

Fresh rosemary to taste

Fresh bay leaves to taste

1/2 cup (100 ml) **white wine**

Chicken broth, as needed

7 oz. (200 g) **hazelnuts (about 1 3/4 cups)**

Cornstarch, as needed

1 lb. (400 g) **broccoli, cut into florets**

Method

Heat the oven to 350°F (175°C).

Sear the turkey in a roasting pan over medium-high heat with half the oil. Season it generously with salt and pepper. Add the onions, carrots, and celery to the pot with a whole clove of garlic and the herbs. Cook for 3 minutes. Add the wine and cook until it evaporates.

Transfer the pan to the oven and roast, occasionally adding a bit of broth, if necessary, until the turkey's internal temperature reaches 165°F (75°C), about 1 hour.

Meanwhile, toast the hazelnuts in a nonstick skillet over medium heat until golden and fragrant.

When the meat is done, remove the garlic and herbs and strain the drippings.

If necessary, add some cornstarch dissolved in a bit of water to thicken the drippings into a gravy.

Add the hazelnuts and let the meat absorb the flavors for a few minutes.

Bring a pan of lightly salted water to a boil and cook the broccoli for 10 minutes. Heat the remaining oil in a skillet over medium and sauté the other garlic clove. Drain the broccoli and add it to the pan. Cook for 5 minutes, smashing it with a spoon. Season with salt and pepper.

Slice the turkey breast and top it with the gravy. Serve it with the smashed broccoli on the side.

Difficulty

CHICKEN MARSALA WITH PEPPERS

POLLO AL MARSALA E PEPERONI

Preparation time: 30 minutes + 30 minutes cooking time

4 Servings

1 chicken (about 4 lbs.),
  cut into 4 pieces
Salt and freshly ground black pepper
  to taste
All-purpose flour, as needed
1/3 cup plus 1 1/2 tbsp. (100 ml)
  extra-virgin olive oil
3 1/2 oz. (100 g) onions
  (about 1 1/2 small), sliced
1 sprig fresh rosemary
3/4 cup plus 1 1/2 tbsp. (200 ml)
  Marsala wine
8 oz. (250 g) red bell peppers
  (about 1 1/2 large), cut into strips
8 oz. (250 g) yellow bell peppers
  (about 1 1/2 large), cut into strips
1 1/4 cups (300 ml) chicken broth
Cornstarch, as needed

Method

Season the chicken with salt and pepper and dredge lightly in flour.

In a large skillet over medium heat, sauté the chicken pieces in two-thirds of the oil until lightly browned.

In a separate pan, sauté the onions with the rosemary in the remaining oil. Add the chicken and the Marsala and cook until the wine evaporates. Add the bell peppers to the pan and let everything finish cooking, occasionally adding broth, as needed, and seasoning with salt and pepper to taste. If you prefer a thicker sauce, dissolve a pinch of cornstarch in a few drops of water and stir into the sauce to combine. Serve.

Did you know that...

Marsala is a fortified wine and is produced in Marsala in the province of Trapani. But how was Marsala born? The most credible version features John Woodhouse, a businessman from Liverpool who was forced by a storm to stop with his ship in the port of Marsala in 1773. During his stay, both he and his crew had the chance to taste the wine produced in the area that was aged in wooden barrels with a method called in perpetuum, which involved topping up the barrels that contained part of the wine from the previous year with wine from the new production. This aging method gave the final product a taste similar to that of the Spanish and Portuguese wines such as Porto and Sherry that, at the time, were much appreciated in the refined drawing rooms of the English nobility. Woodhouse was so fascinated by this wine that he decided to load 50 barrels on board, taking the precaution of adding some wine aquavit to it to increase its alcoholic content in order to maintain its characteristics during the long sea voyage. This Sicilian wine met with such success in England (even today it is stocked in the cellars of Buckingham Palace) that Woodhouse decided to return to Sicily in order to start production and market the product on an industrial scale.

Difficulty

CHICKEN CACCIATORE
POLLO ALLA CACCIATORA

Preparation time: 30 minutes + 30 minutes cooking time

4 Servings

1/3 cup plus 1 1/2 tbsp. (100 ml)
  extra-virgin olive oil
1 chicken (about 4 lbs.),
  cut into 8 pieces
Salt and freshly ground black pepper
  to taste
1 sprig fresh rosemary
1 fresh bay leaf
1 sprig fresh sage
1 onion, thinly sliced
1 carrot, cut into matchsticks
1 stalk celery, cut into matchsticks
1 clove garlic, chopped
3/4 cup plus 1 1/2 tbsp. (200 ml)
  white wine
2 1/4 lbs. (1 kg) ripe tomatoes
  (about 8 medium), seeded
  and cut into small dice
Chicken broth, as needed

Method

Heat 1/4 cup (60 ml) of the oil in a large skillet over medium heat. Season the chicken with salt and pepper. Add the chicken to the skillet and fry until browned.

Tie the rosemary, bay leaf, and sage together with kitchen string.

Heat the remaining oil in a large Dutch oven over medium-low heat. Add the onion, carrot, celery, garlic, and the herb bundle and cook until golden.

Add the chicken and the wine and cook over low heat until the wine evaporates. Add the tomatoes and continue cooking for about 30 minutes, adding enough broth to create a fairly thick sauce. Add more broth, if needed.

When the chicken is thoroughly cooked, remove the bundle of herbs. Serve the chicken with a generous amount of sauce.

Difficulty

SEA BASS IN "ACQUA PAZZA"

BRANZINO ALL'ACQUAPAZZA

Preparation time: 15 minutes + 20 minutes cooking time

4 Servings

3 1/2 tbsp. (50 ml) **extra-virgin olive oil**

5 oz. (150 g) **onions (about 2 small),** thinly sliced

2 **cloves garlic**

5 **fresh basil leaves**

8 oz. (250 g) **cherry tomatoes (about 15)**

3/4 cup plus 1 1/2 tbsp. (200 ml) **water**

3 lbs. 5 oz. (1.5 kg) **sea bass fillets**

Salt and freshly ground black pepper to taste

Method

In a large straight-sided skillet, heat the oil over medium low and sauté the onions, garlic, and basil. Add the tomatoes and water and simmer for 10 minutes.

Season the fish with salt and pepper, then place it, skin side up, in the *acqua pazza* ("crazy water") and cook for 2 minutes. Using two spatulas, gently turn the fillets and simmer for 5 minutes until flaky and cooked through.

Did you know that...

Acqua pazza (literally, "crazy water") was originally a sort of traditional maritime soup. Fishermen would take the small discarded fish that remained tangled in the nets (and therefore went unsold) and boil them in seawater with vegetables and spices. The recipe got its name, which is still used today, when a bit of white wine was added to the water. Popular throughout the Mediterranean, especially in Provence and southern Italy, it was a frugal yet wholesome one-course meal usually eaten with hard tack biscuits called gallette *or* friselle. *It's important to note that every region of Italy offers fish dishes modeled on this basic soup – water, salt, and spices, occasionally enriched with eggs, cheese, scraps of meat, or bones, depending on the traditional products available in the area.*

Difficulty

BAKED SEA BASS

BRANZINO AL FORNO

Preparation time: 20 minutes + 12 to 15 minutes cooking time

4 to 6 Servings

Salt and freshly ground black pepper
  to taste

7 oz. (200 g) potatoes,
  peeled and cut into wedges

2 whole sea bass, about
  1 1/3 lbs. (500 to 600 g) each,
  filleted

20 small black olives, preferably
  Taggiasca

2 oz. (80 g) salt-packed capers,
  rinsed well and drained

4 sprigs fresh rosemary

4 fresh sage leaves

1/3 cup plus 1 1/2 tbsp. (100 ml)
  extra-virgin olive oil

1 tbsp. (4 g) chopped fresh parsley

Method

Bring a large pot of salted water to a boil and cook the potatoes for 5 minutes; drain.

Meanwhile, heat the oven to 350°F (175°C).

Place four parchment squares on a work surface. Divide the fish fillets among the parchment squares and season with salt and pepper. Distribute the olives, capers, and potato wedges over the sea bass. Top each fillet with the rosemary and sage. Drizzle with the oil and fold the parchment over the fish, folding and crimping the edges tightly to seal and enclose the filling completely.

Wrap the paper packets individually in aluminum foil and bake for 12 to 15 minutes. Serve the sea bass fillets with a sprinkling of parsley.

Difficulty

MUSSELS MARINARA

COZZE ALLA MARINARA

Preparation time: 20 minutes + 5 minutes cooking time

4 Servings

2 1/4 lbs. (1 kg) **mussels**
1/4 cup (60 ml) **extra-virgin olive oil,**
 plus more for drizzling
Crushed red pepper flakes to taste
1 **clove garlic, minced**
Fresh parsley to taste, chopped
1/2 cup (100 ml) **white wine**
7 oz. (200 g) **tomatoes**
 (about 2 small), peeled,
 seeded, and diced
Salt to taste

Method

Thoroughly soak, clean, and debeard the mussels, rinsing well to remove all sand and grit.

Heat the oil in a large sauté pan over medium. Add the crushed red pepper flakes, garlic, and parsley and cook until fragrant.

Add the white wine and cook until it evaporates. Add the tomatoes to the pan and, after a few minutes, add the mussels and let them cook until they open, about 10 minutes; discard any that do not open.

Season with salt, if necessary. Serve with a drizzle of olive oil.

Did you know that...

Wine was "discovered" several millennia ago – the Bible presents Noah as the first wine grower in human history – and found its place in the Mediterranean region. Ancient wine was fortified, spiced, dense, and thick with added fragrances. It was definitely a long way from the wine we know today. This precious and intoxicating drink is an almost essential complement to an Italian meal, but it's also a food product itself and a primary ingredient in numerous recipes. The Romans spread the custom of producing and drinking wine to the north, far beyond the confines of the peninsula, where it bumped into the beer cultures of England and Germany. At the time "white winemaking" was preferred, which resulted in a fortified product that was very high in alcohol and resin. The Benedictine monks made the more natural "red winemaking" process popular, probably because of the analogy between the color of blood and the color of the drink, which was essential for celebrating the Christian liturgy. The role of wine in modern cooking can be compared to that of a sauce – its purpose is to enhance the food to which it is added.

Difficulty

SWORDFISH IN SALMORIGLIO SAUCE

PESCE SPADA AL SALMORIGLIO

Preparation time: 15 minutes + 5 minutes cooking time

4 Servings

1 cup (200 ml) **extra-virgin olive oil**
Juice of 2 lemons
3 1/2 tbsp. (50 ml) **hot water**
1 **clove garlic, chopped**
1 tbsp. (4 g) **fresh parsley, chopped**
1 tsp. **fresh oregano, chopped**
1 1/3 lbs. (600 g) **swordfish fillet,** cut into four slices
Salt and freshly ground black pepper to taste

Method

Make the salmoriglio sauce: Whisk together the oil, lemon juice, and water in a medium bowl. Add the garlic, parsley, and oregano. Emulsify the sauce: Place the bowl over a pan of gently simmering water, whisking constantly, for 5 to 6 minutes.

Brush the slices of fish with the salmoriglio sauce and cook on a medium-high griddle or grill for 4 to 5 minutes per side, moistening it with the sauce as the fish cooks. Season with salt and pepper.

Brush with the sauce once again and serve.

Did you know that...

Swordfish is a typical Sicilian dish, as is the salmoriglio sauce with which it is served. This traditional sauce, whose name is the Italian adaptation of the Sicilian term sammurigghiu, *usually accompanies grilled meat or fish.*
Swordfish is caught in the area around the Straits of Messina and is a prized symbol of Sicilian and Calabrian cuisine. In these regions, this prized fish is eaten roasted, smoked, or marinated or in carpaccio. It seems that fishing for swordfish in this small stretch of sea was done even in prehistoric times. Indeed, swordfish bones, among the remains of food, were discovered in ruins of villages dating back to the Bronze Age.

Difficulty

GROUPER MATALOTTA-STYLE

CERNIA ALLA MATALOTTA

Preparation time: 25 minutes + 15 minutes cooking time

4 Servings

1/2 cup (60 g) **all-purpose flour**

1 3/4 lbs. (800 g) **grouper fillets**

3 1/2 tbsp. (50 ml) **extra-virgin olive oil**

3 1/2 oz. (100 g) **onions (about 1 1/2 small), thinly sliced**

1 **clove garlic, thinly sliced**

1/2 cup (100 ml) **white wine**

7 oz. (200 g) **tomatoes (about 2 small), quartered**

1/2 cup (100 ml) **fish broth**

1 **fresh bay leaf**

3 1/2 oz. (100 g) **button mushrooms, thinly sliced**

Salt and freshly ground black pepper to taste

1/3 oz. (8 g) **fresh parsley, chopped**

FOR THE TOPPING

3 1/2 oz. (100 g) **zucchini (about 1/2 medium), sliced**

2 3/4 oz. (80 g) **bell peppers (about 1 small), cut into small dice**

1/4 cup (30 g) **slivered almonds**

Difficulty

Method

Place the flour in a baking pan with low edges. Lightly flour the grouper fillets.

Heat the oil in a large skillet and sauté half of the onions and the garlic for 1 minute over medium. Add the fish and fry gently. Add the white wine and simmer until it evaporates.

Add the tomatoes, fish broth, bay leaf, and mushrooms, and season with salt and pepper. Add the parsley and cook over low heat for 5 minutes.

Make the topping: In a medium skillet over high heat, sauté the remaining onions, the zucchini, and a pinch of salt. Add the bell peppers and cook until tender. Season to taste. Stir in the almonds.

Arrange the fillets on a serving dish, then top with the vegetables and serve.

POTATO-CRUSTED SNAPPER
DENTICE IN CROSTA DI PATATE

Preparation time: 30 minutes + 15 to 20 minutes cooking time

4 Servings

2 1/4 lbs. (1 kg) **red snapper**
12 oz. (350 g) **potatoes**
Salt and freshly ground black pepper
3 tbsp. (40 ml) **extra-virgin olive oil,**
  plus more for baking pan

Method

Clean, scale, rinse, and fillet the snapper.

Peel the potatoes. Using a mandoline, slice the potatoes into thin rounds, then blanch them in a large pot of boiling salted water for 1 minute.

Heat the oven to 400°F (200°C). Grease a 9- by 13-inch (23 by 33 cm) baking pan (or line it with parchment paper). Place the snapper fillets in the pan, letting them overlap. Season with salt and pepper, cover with the potato rounds, overlapping them slightly as well. Drizzle with the olive oil and bake for 15 to 20 minutes.

Did you know that...

In the early Christian era marked by famine, it seems strange that 140-160 days of the year should be for fasting. With the growth of Christianity, a series of norms (initially reserved for hermits and monks, then extended to everyone) also spread, which regulated all aspects of daily life including diet. The "eating lean" requirement made it obligatory to abstain from certain foods (especially red meat and animal fats) on certain days: Wednesdays and Fridays, along with the eves of religious festivals (Christmas and Easter, to name the most important ones) and the period of Lent. Religious liturgy very strongly conditioned Italian eating habits. For example, the opposition between fish and meat, which didn't exist in other cultures (not even ancient Rome), came to be perceived as natural. It also developed two parallel alimentary traditions: one of "lean" foods (fish, oil, vegetables, limited white meat) and another of "fatty" foods (red meat, lard, cold cuts). Cookbooks specified whether each dish belonged to one category or the other at least until the 19th century.

Difficulty

JUMBO SHRIMP WITH TOMATO CONFIT
MILLEFOGLIE DI CANOCCHIE E POMODORI CONFIT

Preparation time: 1 hour 30 minutes + 2 hours resting time + 6 minutes cooking time

4 Servings

24 **jumbo shrimp**
Salt and freshly ground black pepper
  to taste
3 1/2 tbsp. (50 ml) **extra-virgin**
  olive oil
2 1/2 lbs. (1.2 kg) **tomatoes (about**
  6 large)
1/3 oz. (10 g) **chopped fresh thyme**
  (about 1/4 cup)
1 **clove garlic, thinly sliced**
Sugar to taste
1 oz. (30 g) **fresh basil**
  (about 1 1/4 cups whole leaves)
3 1/2 oz. (100 g) **mixed greens**

Method

Clean and shell the jumbo shrimp. Season them with salt, pepper, and 2 tablespoons (25 ml) of the oil and let them marinate for 2 hours.

Heat the oven to 175°F (80°C). Prepare the tomatoes by making an X-shaped incision on the bottom of each tomato and blanching them in boiling water for 10 to 15 seconds. Immediately dip the tomatoes in ice water, then peel them, cut them into quarters, and remove the seeds. Place them on a parchment-lined baking sheet. Season them on both sides with thyme, garlic, and a pinch of salt, pepper, and sugar. Bake for 1 hour.

Raise the oven temperature to 300°F (150°C). Arrange 4 ramekins on a parchment-lined baking pan. Fill them with alternating layers of tomatoes and shrimp, finishing with a layer of tomatoes. Bake for 6 minutes.

Blanch the basil leaves in a small amount of boiling salted water for 2 minutes. Drain the basil and put it directly in a bowl of ice water. Use an immersion blender to blend them with the remaining oil. Remove the ramekins from the oven and serve the shrimp and tomatoes drizzled with the basil oil with mixed greens.

Difficulty

OVEN-BAKED MUSSELS, POTATOES, AND RICE

TIELLA DI PATATE, RISO, E COZZE

Preparation time: 30 minutes + 45 minutes cooking time

4 Servings

1 1/3 lbs. (600 g) **mussels**

12 oz. (350 g) **cherry tomatoes (about 21)**

1/3 cup plus 1 1/2 tbsp. (100 ml) **extra-virgin olive oil**

6 oz. (180 g) **onions (about 2 large), sliced**

1 **clove garlic, minced**

2 tbsp. (8 g) **chopped parsley**

Salt and freshly ground black pepper to taste

3 oz. (85 g) **Pecorino cheese, grated**

11 oz. (300 g) **potatoes, peeled and sliced**

8 oz. (250 g) **long-grain rice, rinsed and drained**

2 to 2 1/2 cups (500 to 600 ml) **water**

Method

Thoroughly soak, clean, and debeard the mussels, rinsing well to remove all sand and grit. Open the mussels using a small knife. This operation should be performed over a container to collect the liquid. Set the liquid aside. Discard any empty shells.

Cut half the cherry tomatoes into wedges and leave the rest whole.

Heat the oven to 350°F (175°C). Drizzle 1 1/2 tablespoons (20 ml) of the olive oil into the bottom of a 9- by 13-inch (23 by 33 cm) baking dish. Arrange a layer of the onions in the baking dish and scatter with half the garlic, parsley, and cherry tomatoes. Season with salt and pepper, sprinkle half the grated Pecorino over the top, and finish with half the sliced potatoes. Cover with all of the rice, then arrange the mussels over the top. Make another layer with the rest of the garlic, parsley, and cherry tomatoes and cover with the remaining potatoes. Season again with salt and pepper. Sprinkle with the remaining grated Pecorino and drizzle with the remaining olive oil.

Pour in the liquid reserved from the mussels, adding water to completely cover the ingredients. Bake the casserole (referred to in Italian as a *tiella*) for about 45 minutes, or until the rice is cooked completely.

Difficulty

EGGPLANT PARMIGIANA
PARMIGIANA DI MELANZANE

Preparation time: 30 minutes + 1 hour cooking time

4 Servings

1 lb. (500 g) **eggplant (about 1 medium), thinly sliced**

Salt to taste

1/2 cup plus 2 tbsp. (80 g) **all-purpose flour**

2 **large eggs, beaten**

Vegetable oil, as needed

11 oz. (300 g) **tomato sauce**

3 oz. (100 g) **mozzarella cheese, shredded**

3 oz. (100 g) **pork sausages, casings removed and crumbled**

3 oz. (100 g) **Parmigiano Reggiano cheese, grated (about 1 cup)**

Method

Slice the eggplant, then put it in a colander, salt it lightly, and allow it to drain for about 30 minutes.

Heat the oven to 350°F (175°C). Dredge the eggplant slices in flour and then dip in the egg. Heat the vegetable oil in a skillet until hot and shimmering. Fry the eggplant until golden-brown on both sides. Transfer to a plate lined with paper towels to drain.

Pour a thin layer of tomato sauce in the bottom of a 9- by 13-inch (23 by 33 cm) baking dish, then arrange a layer of eggplant slices. Cover with mozzarella and sausage, then add some tomato sauce, and sprinkle with Parmigiano Reggiano. Add another layer of eggplant, repeating the layering of ingredients until all but a small amount of sauce and Parmigiano are used (the last layer must be of eggplant slices). Top with the sauce and Parmigiano Reggiano. Bake until the top has formed a golden crust, about 25 minutes. Let rest for 15 minutes before serving.

Note: You can substitute zucchini for the eggplant if you wish. The preparation is the same, but the zucchini must be sliced lengthwise. You can also replace the sausage with a layer of sliced Mortadella.

Difficulty

STUFFED PEPPERS

PEPERONI RIPIENI

Preparation time: 30 minutes + 25 minutes cooking time

4 Servings

4 bell peppers

8 1/2 oz. (240 g) **fresh breadcrumbs**

Salt and freshly ground black pepper
  to taste

Fresh basil leaves, torn

1 3/4 oz. (50 g) **Caciocavallo cheese**
  or Provolone, grated (about 1/2 cup)

2 tbsp. **capers**

4 **tomatoes**

4 **salted anchovies, desalted, deboned,**
  and chopped

Extra-virgin olive oil, as needed

Unsalted butter, for baking dish

Method

Heat the oven to 400°F (200°C).

Remove the stalks, ribs, and seeds of the peppers, taking care not to break them. Cut them in half.

In a skillet over medium heat, brown the breadcrumbs lightly and season with the salt, pepper, and plenty of basil. Add the Caciocavallo, capers, tomatoes and anchovies. Mix well, drizzling with enough olive oil to bind the mixture. Stuff the peppers with the breadcrumb mixture.

Place the peppers in a buttered baking dish, add a little oil, cover with aluminum foil, and bake for 15 minutes. Remove the aluminum foil and cook for another 10 minutes, drizzling with more oil if necessary. Serve lukewarm or at room temperature.

Difficulty

PUMPKIN CURRY
CURRY DI ZUCCA

Preparation time: 15 minutes + 20 minutes cooking time

4 Servings

1 lb. 5 oz. (600 g) **pumpkin**
1 tbsp. (15 ml) **extra-virgin olive oil**
3 1/2 oz. (100 g) **onions**
  (about 1 1/2 small), sliced
2 tbsp. (13 g) **curry powder or paste**
2 1/2 cups (500 ml) **milk**
  or 2 cups (500 ml) **coconut milk**
Salt

Method

Wash the pumpkin. Peel and seed it and remove the filaments. Cut it into 1/2- to 1-inch (1 to 2 cm) cubes.

In a large skillet, heat the oil over medium low and sauté the onions until softened. Add the curry powder or paste and stir to combine.

Add the milk, bring to a boil over medium heat, add the diced pumpkin, and season with salt. Simmer for about 20 minutes, or until the pumpkin is tender and the sauce has thickened to a desired consistency.

Did you know that...

Pumpkins are not of Italian origin, but they were adopted and assimilated well, and the many varieties were used in all kinds of wonderful recipes. Their sweetness made them particularly ideal for stuffed pastas, or sweet-and-sour and sweet-and-spicy sauces. After the Americas were discovered and various species were imported (larger and with more pulp than native varieties), the timid use of pumpkin for cooking began, mostly in the northern rural areas. Pumpkin tortelli are still an obligatory "lean" first course for the traditional Christmas Eve dinner in many families, especially in the Po Valley.

Difficulty

ZUCCHINI PARMESAN
PARMIGIANA DI ZUCCHINE

Preparation time: 1 hour + 20 minutes cooking time

4 Servings

FOR THE TOMATO SAUCE

1 1/2 tbsp. (20 ml) **extra-virgin olive oil**

1 **clove garlic**

11 oz. (300 g) **crushed tomatoes (about 2 medium)**

Salt and freshly ground black pepper to taste

1 lb. 5 oz. (600 g) **zucchini (about 3 medium)**

5 oz. (150 g) **mozzarella**

Extra-virgin olive oil, for frying

1/3 cup plus 1 tbsp. (50 g) **all-purpose flour**

2 **large eggs, lightly beaten**

11 oz. (300 g) **tomato sauce**

Fresh basil leaves to taste, torn

3 oz. (100 g) **Parmigiano Reggiano cheese, grated (about 1 cup)**

Salt to taste

Method

Make the tomato sauce: Heat the oil in a large skillet over low heat. Peel the garlic and cook in the oil for 3 to 4 minutes, making sure it doesn't brown. Add the crushed tomatoes, season with salt and pepper, and cook over medium heat for 20 minutes.

Assemble the dish: Very thinly slice the zucchini lengthwise, about 1/8 inch (3 mm) thick. Thinly slice the mozzarella.

Heat about 1/2 inch (1.5 cm) of olive oil in a pan until it is shimmering. Dredge the zucchini slices in flour, then dip them in the egg, and fry them. Use a slotted spoon to transfer them to paper towels to drain. Sprinkle zucchini with salt.

Heat the oven to 350°F (175°C). Spread a thin layer of tomato sauce in a baking dish. Cover it with a layer of fried zucchini, then one of mozzarella. Follow with another layer of tomato sauce. Sprinkle with the basil and Parmigiano. Arrange another layer of zucchini and continue in the same order (ending with a layer of zucchini) until all the ingredients have been used.

Cover with sauce and Parmigiano, then bake until the surface is golden and bubbling. Let cool for at least 15 minutes and serve.

Difficulty

ROASTED VEGETABLE MEDLEY WITH PECORINO TOSCANO

MOSAICO DI VERDURE CON PECORINO TOSCANO

Preparation time: 30 minutes + 1 hour resting time + 20 minutes cooking time

4 Servings

8 oz. (250 g) **eggplant**
(about 1/2 medium)

6 oz. (160 g) **carrots**
(about 2 1/2 medium)

5 oz. (150 g) **red onions, preferably
Tropea** (about 2 small)

7 oz. (200 g) **zucchini**
(about 1 medium)

4 oz. (120 g) **tomatoes**
(about 1 medium)

7 oz. (200 g) **yellow bell peppers**
(about 2 medium)

7 oz. (200 g) **red bell peppers**
(about 2 medium)

3 1/2 tbsp. (50 ml) **extra-virgin
olive oil** (preferably from Tuscany),
plus more for drizzling

Salt to taste

Fresh basil leaves to taste, torn

4 oz. (100 g) **Pecorino cheese**
(preferably from Tuscany)

Difficulty

Method

Slice the eggplant, carrots, onions, and zucchini. Cut the tomato into wedges.

Grill the sliced vegetables and the whole bell peppers. Peel the peppers and cut lengthwise into strips (discarding seeds and ribs). Place all the vegetables in a bowl with the olive oil, a pinch of salt, and the basil. Let them marinate for at least 1 hour.

Grate or thinly shave the Pecorino. Arrange the vegetables on a serving plate. Sprinkle the cheese over the top. Drizzle with olive oil and garnish with fresh basil leaves, if desired.

Did you know that...

The typical Italian predilection for mixed greens, salads and vegetables (raw or cooked) is unquestionable. But reading various works from the past brings another aspect to light, one that is not given enough attention. Vegetable preparation methods, various modes of consumption (even types of chewing) and traditional seasonings and dressings are all based on cultural factors. Bartolomeo Sacchi, also called Platina, was a 15th century humanist and gastronomer. In his treatise De Honesta Voluptate, *he describes the Italian dressing par excellence at length and in great detail: First a generous dose of salt, then high quality oil (distributed generously by hand), followed by a dash of good vinegar. After mixing thoroughly, the vegetables should be left to macerate, allowing the flavors and aromas to mingle to perfection. It's no coincidence that grapes and olives, elements of the famous Mediterranean triad (which includes tomatoes), are combined in even the simplest of condiments.*

PIZZA & FOCACCIA

CHAPTER FIVE

FOUR-CHEESE PIZZA

PIZZA AI QUATTRO FORMAGGI

Preparation time: 15 minutes + 1 1/2 to 6 hours rising time + 20 minutes cooking time

4 Servings

FOR THE DOUGH

4 cups (500 g) **all-purpose flour or italian "00" flour, plus more as needed**

1 1/2 tsp. (4 g) **active dry yeast for 1 1/2-hour rising time** or 3/4 tsp. (2 g) **for 6-hour rising time**

1 1/2 cups (350 ml) **lukewarm water**

1 1/2 tbsp. (20 ml) **extra-virgin olive oil**

2 tsp. (12 g) **salt**

FOR THE TOPPING

1 **16-oz. can peeled tomatoes, crushed by hand**

3 1/2 oz. (100 g) **Gorgonzola cheese, crumbled**

3 1/2 oz. (100 g) **Fontina cheese, shredded**

3 1/2 oz. (100 g) **Brie cheese, diced**

3 1/2 oz. (100 g) **smoked Scamorza or mozzarella cheese, shredded**

Method

Make the dough: Put the flour on a clean work surface and make a well in the center. Dissolve the yeast in the water and pour the yeast mixture into the well. Gradually incorporate the yeast mixture into the flour until a loose dough starts to form, then add the oil and salt. Knead the dough until it is smooth and elastic. Cover the dough with lightly oiled plastic wrap, and let it rest for about 10 minutes.

Assemble the pizza: Grease a 12-inch (30 cm) round pizza pan with oil. Transfer the dough to the pan and, using your fingertips, spread the dough to cover the bottom of the pan.

If you used 1 1/2 teaspoons (4 g) of yeast, let the dough rise for about 40 minutes. If, on the other hand, you used 3/4 teaspoon (2 g), then cover the dough with a sheet of lightly oiled plastic wrap and refrigerate for at least 5 hours. The dough will rise perfectly well in the refrigerator, becoming light and fragrant.

Top with the tomatoes and sprinkle with the cheeses (all at room temperature). Let the dough rise for 40 minutes more. Bake at 425°F (220°C) for 20 minutes, or until the cheese is bubbly and the crust is golden-brown.

Difficulty

APULIAN-STYLE PIZZA
PIZZA ALLA PUGLIESE

Preparation time: 15 minutes + 1 1/2 to 6 hours rising time + 20 minutes cooking time

4 Servings

FOR THE DOUGH

4 cups (500 g) **all-purpose flour or italian "00" flour, plus more as needed**

1 1/2 tsp. (4 g) **active dry yeast for 1 1/2-hour rising time** or 3/4 tsp. (2 g) **for 6-hour rising time**

1 1/2 cups (350 ml) **lukewarm water**

1 1/2 tbsp. (20 ml) **extra-virgin olive oil**

2 tsp. (12 g) **salt**

FOR THE TOPPING

1 **16-oz. can peeled tomatoes, crushed by hand**

7 slices Caciocavallo or Provolone cheese

11 oz. (300 g) yellow onions (about 2 medium), sliced

10 pitted green and black olives, sliced

Fresh oregano (optional)

Method

Make the dough: Put the flour on a clean work surface and make a well in the center. Dissolve the yeast in the water and pour the yeast mixture into the well. Gradually incorporate the yeast mixture into the flour until a loose dough starts to form, then add the oil and salt. Knead the dough until it is smooth and elastic. Cover the dough with lightly oiled plastic wrap, and let it rest for about 10 minutes.

Assemble the pizza: Grease a 12-inch (30 cm) round pizza pan with oil. Transfer the dough to the pan and, using your fingertips, spread the dough to cover the bottom of the pan.

If you used 1 1/2 teaspoons (4 g) of yeast, let the dough rise for about 40 minutes. If, on the other hand, you used 3/4 teaspoon (2 g), then cover the dough with a sheet of lightly oiled plastic wrap and refrigerate for at least 5 hours. The dough will rise perfectly well in the refrigerator, becoming light and fragrant.

Top the dough with the tomatoes, the Caciocavallo or Provolone, onions, and olives (all at room temperature). Let the dough rise for 40 minutes more. Bake at 425°F (220°C) for 20 minutes, or until the cheese is bubbly and the crust is golden-brown. Garnish with oregano, if desired.

Difficulty

PIZZA WITH EGGPLANT AND PROVOLA CHEESE

PIZZA CON MELANZANE E PROVOLA

Preparation time: 30 minutes + 1 1/2 to 5 hours rising time + 8 minutes cooking time

4 Servings

FOR THE DOUGH

5 cups (650 g) **all-purpose flour
or Italian "00" flour,
plus more as needed**
3/4 tsp. (2 g) **active dry yeast**
1 1/2 cups plus 1 tsp. (375 ml)
lukewarm water
1 tbsp. (18 g) **salt**

FOR THE TOPPING

1 lb. (500 g) **crushed tomatoes
(about 4 medium)**
Salt to taste
Extra-virgin olive oil
11 oz. (300 g) **eggplant
(about 1/2 large)**
9 oz. (250 g) **Pachino
or cherry tomatoes**
1 lb. (500 g) **Sicilian Provola
(or Fontina or Pecorino) cheese,
thinly sliced**

Method

Make the dough: Put the flour on a clean work surface and make a well in the center. Dissolve the yeast in the water and pour the yeast mixture into the well. Gradually incorporate the yeast mixture into the flour until a loose dough starts to form, then add the salt. Knead the dough until it is smooth and elastic. Cover the dough with a sheet of lightly oiled plastic wrap and let rise until doubled in volume (from 1 to 4 hours, depending on the room temperature).

Divide the dough into four portions and roll them into balls. Let them rise again, covered with lightly oiled plastic wrap, until they again double in size (from 30 minutes to 1 hour, depending on the room temperature).

Assemble the pizza: Season the crushed tomatoes with salt and a dash of olive oil. Slice and grill the eggplant, or fry the slices in olive oil, then drain. Halve the Pachino or cherry tomatoes.

Sprinkle the work surface with flour and flatten each dough ball, starting with your fingertips and progressing to a rotary movement of your hands as the dough gets flatter and wider, into a round about 8 inches (20 cm) in diameter.

Put the dough rounds on a baking sheet. Spread the crushed tomatoes over each pizza and arrange the tomatoes, eggplant, and cheese on top.

Bake at 500°F (250°C) for 8 minutes, or until the cheese is bubbly and the crust is golden-brown.

Difficulty

PIZZA WITH ARUGULA AND PARMIGIANO REGGIANO CHEESE
PIZZA CON RUCOLA E PARMIGIANO REGGIANO

Preparation time: 15 minutes + 1 1/2 to 6 hours rising time + 20 minutes cooking time

4 Servings

FOR THE DOUGH

4 cups (500 g) all-purpose flour or italian "00" flour, plus more as needed

1 1/2 tsp. (4 g) active dry yeast for 1 1/2-hour rising time or 3/4 tsp. (2 g) for 6-hour rising time

1 1/2 cups (350 ml) lukewarm water

1 1/2 tbsp. (20 ml) extra-virgin olive oil

2 tsp. (12 g) salt

FOR THE TOPPING

1 16-oz. can medium peeled tomatoes, crushed by hand

14 oz. (400 g) mozzarella cheese, thinly sliced

4 oz. (113 g) baby arugula, chopped

5 1/4 oz. (150 g) Parmigiano Reggiano cheese, grated (about 1 1/2 cup)

Method

Make the dough: Put the flour on a clean work surface and make a well in the center. Dissolve the yeast in the water and pour the yeast mixture into the well. Gradually incorporate the yeast mixture into the flour until a loose dough starts to form, then add the oil and salt. Knead the dough until it is smooth and elastic. Cover the dough with lightly oiled plastic wrap, and let it rest for about 10 minutes.

Assemble the pizza: Grease a 12-inch (30 cm) round pizza pan with oil. Transfer the dough to the pan and, using your fingertips, spread the dough to cover the bottom of the pan.

If you used 1 1/2 teaspoons (4 g) of yeast, let the dough rise for about 40 minutes. If, on the other hand, you used 3/4 teaspoon (2 g), then cover the dough with a sheet of lightly oiled plastic wrap and refrigerate for at least 5 hours. The dough will rise perfectly well in the refrigerator, becoming light and fragrant.

Spread the tomatoes over the dough and top with the mozzarella (at room temperature). Garnish with the arugula and Parmigiano Reggiano (at room temperature). Let the dough rise for 40 minutes more. Bake at 425°F (220°C) for 20 minutes, or until the cheese is bubbly and the crust is golden-brown.

Difficulty

SICILIAN PIZZA

SFINCIONE

Preparation time: 30 minutes + 1 1/2 hours rising time + 25 minutes cooking time

4 Servings

FOR THE DOUGH

2 cups (250 g) all-purpose flour or
   Italian "00" flour, plus more as needed
2 cups (250 g) durum wheat
   or semolina flour
2 1/4 tsp. (6 g) active dry yeast
1 cup (250 ml) lukewarm water
1 1/4 tsp. (5 g) sugar
3 1/2 tbsp. (50 ml) extra-virgin
   olive oil
2 tsp. (12 g) salt

FOR THE TOPPING

3 medium tomatoes, peeled, seeded,
   and finely chopped
Salt and freshly ground black pepper
   to taste
3 1/2 tbsp. (50 ml) extra-virgin
   olive oil
1 medium onion, finely chopped
Fresh oregano, chopped
8 anchovies, rinsed or in oil
3 1/2 oz. (100 g) semi-seasoned
   Caciocavallo or Provolone cheese,
   grated

Difficulty

Method

Make the dough: Mix the flours on a clean work surface and make a well in the center. Dissolve the yeast in the water and pour the yeast mixture into the well. Gradually incorporate the yeast mixture into the flour until a loose dough starts to form. Add the sugar and the oil and, lastly, the salt dissolved in 3 tablespoons (50 ml) of water. Knead the dough until it is smooth and elastic. Cover the dough with lightly oiled plastic wrap, and let it rise until doubled in volume, about 1 hour.

Make the topping and assemble the pizza: In a bowl, toss the tomatoes with the salt, pepper, and oil. Stir in the onion and a pinch of oregano.

Grease a 12-inch (30 cm) round pizza pan with oil. Transfer the dough to the pan and, using your fingertips, spread the dough to cover the bottom of the pan.

Cover the dough with the tomato mixture, the anchovies, and the cheese. Let it rise for at least 30 minutes.

Bake at 450°F (230°C) for 25 minutes, or until the cheese is bubbly and the crust is golden-brown.

SAGE FOCACCIA
FOCACCIA ALLA SALVIA

Preparation time: 15 minutes + 1 1/2 hours rising time + 25 minutes cooking time

4 Servings

FOR THE DOUGH

4 cups (500 g) **all-purpose flour**
1 1/2 tsp. (4 g) **active dry yeast**
1 cup (250 ml) **lukewarm water**
1 tbsp. (18 g) **malt**
  or 1/2 tbsp. (10 g) **honey**
10 **fresh sage leaves, finely chopped**
2 tbsp. plus 2 tsp. (40 ml) **extra-virgin olive oil**
1 1/2 tsp. (10 g) **salt**

FOR THE GENOESE BRINE

1/2 cup (100 ml) **water**
3 1/2 tbsp. (50 ml) **extra-virgin olive oil**
2 1/4 tsp. (14 g) **coarse salt**

Method

Make the dough: Put the flour on a clean work surface and make a well in the center. Dissolve the yeast in the water and pour the yeast mixture and malt or honey into the well. Gradually incorporate them into the flour. Add the sage and the oil. Lastly, add the salt and knead the dough until it is soft, smooth, and elastic. Cover the dough with a sheet of lightly oiled plastic wrap, and let it rise in a warm place until doubled in volume, about 30 minutes.

Make the brine: Combine the water, oil, and salt in a bowl. Stir to make an emulsion and then let it rest.

Transfer the dough to a lightly oiled baking pan, stretching it gently with your fingertips. Prod the surface of the dough with your fingers, forming small dimples where the seasoning will collect. Sprinkle the focaccia with the brine and let it rise until it has doubled in volume, about 1 hour.

Bake at 400°F (200°C) for about 25 minutes, or until the crust is golden-brown.

Difficulty

FOCACCIA FROM APULIA

FOCACCIA PUGLIESE

Preparation time: 15 minutes + 3 1/2 hours rising time + 20 minutes cooking time

4 Servings

FOR THE DOUGH

3 oz. (80 g) **potatoes**
  (about 1 1/2 small)
4 cups (500 g) **all-purpose flour**
1 cup (170 g) **semolina flour**
2 1/4 tbsp. (6 g) **active dry yeast**
1 2/3 cups (400 ml) **lukewarm water**
2 1/2 tsp. (15 g) **salt**
1/4 cup plus 1 tsp. (65 ml) **extra-virgin olive oil**

FOR THE TOPPING

7 oz. (200 g) **cherry tomatoes, halved**
Coarse salt
Olive oil
Dried oregano

Method

Put the potatoes in a saucepan and cover with cold water. Bring to a boil and cook until tender, about 15 minutes. Drain the potatoes, let cool slightly, and mash them.

Combine the two types of flours on a clean work surface and make a well in the center. Dissolve the yeast in 1 cup (240 ml) of the water. Pour the yeast mixture into the well and gradually incorporate it into the flour. Add the salt, oil, mashed potatoes, and, gradually, the remaining water. Knead the dough until it is soft, smooth, and elastic.

Divide the dough into 4 balls. Cover the dough with a sheet of lightly oiled plastic wrap and let it rise until doubled in volume, about 3 hours.

Flip the dough balls over and spread each with your fingertips to cover the bottom of each pan. Top each with the tomatoes, a pinch of salt, a drizzle of olive oil, and a sprinkle of oregano.

Let them rise again until doubled in volume, about 30 minutes.

Bake at 450°F (230°C) for 25 minutes, or until the crust is golden-brown.

Difficulty

SIDE DISHES

CHAPTER SIX

ROASTED POTATOES WITH TOMATOES AND ONIONS

PATATE AL FORNO CON POMODORI E CIPOLLE

Preparation time: 20 minutes + 20 minutes cooking time

4 Servings

1 1/3 lbs. (600 g) **potatoes**
(about 3 medium)

14 oz. (400 g) **tomatoes**
(about 4 small)

11 oz. (300 g) **yellow onions**
(about 2 medium)

**Salt and freshly ground black pepper
to taste**

3 tbsp. (40 ml) **extra-virgin olive oil**

1 1/2 oz. (40 g) **Pecorino cheese,**
grated (about 1/3 cup plus 1 tbsp.)

Method

Scrub and peel the potatoes. Cut them into rounds about 1/8 inch (3 mm) thick and place them in a bowl of cold water. Slice the tomatoes into rounds about 1/4 inch (5 mm) thick. Peel the onions and slice them into rings 1/10 inch (2 mm) thick.

Heat the oven to 350°F (175°C). Arrange the potatoes, tomatoes, and onions in layers in a parchment-lined baking pan, alternating the ingredients until they have all been used. Season with salt and pepper. Finish with a drizzle of olive oil and a sprinkling of Pecorino.

Bake for about 20 minutes, or until all the vegetables are fork-tender. Cover with aluminum foil if the vegetables become too dry during cooking.

Did you know that...

Italy was the first European country after Spain to become acquainted with the tomato. This occurred because of the close relationship between the ruling families of the time and the Spanish dominions that existed on Italian territory. The tomato's "official" history in Italy started in Pisa on October 31, 1548, when the Grand Duke of Tuscany, Cosimo de' Medici, received a crate a tomatoes from the Florentine estate of Torre de Gallo; the seeds had probably been a gift from the viceroy of Naples to his daughter, Eleonora of Toledo, Cosimo's wife. From Sardinia, still ruled by Spain, the tomato reached Genoa, at the time the main port of the Tyrrhenian Sea. From there it spread throughout Liguria thanks to the favorable climate. The tomato then crossed the Apennines and reached the plains of Piacenza, Parma, Milan, Novara, and Turin.

Difficulty

SAVORY PUMPKIN PIE

TORTA SALATA DI ZUCCA

Preparation time: 1 hour + 30 minutes cooking time

4 Servings

1 lb. 11 oz. (750 g) **pumpkin**
2 **large eggs**
3/4 cup (80 g) **grated Parmigiano Reggiano cheese**
1/2 cup (125 ml) **fresh cream**
Salt and freshly ground black pepper to taste
Freshly grated nutmeg
11 oz. (300 g) **puff pastry**

Method

Heat the oven to 350°F (175°C). Wash the pumpkin, cut it into large pieces, and bake it in a large baking pan for 30 minutes, or until it is tender. If it begins to over-brown, cover it with aluminum foil. Let the pumpkin cool, then scrape out and discard the seeds and filaments.

Purée the pumpkin in a blender. Transfer it to a bowl and add the eggs, Parmigiano, and cream. Season with salt, pepper, and a dash of grated nutmeg.

Heat the oven to 350°F (175°C). Roll out the puff pastry to 1/8 inch (3 mm) thick and transfer to a pie pan. Using your fingers, spread the pastry into the corners and up the sides of the pan. Pour in the pumpkin mixture and smooth the surface. Bake for 30 minutes, or until golden-brown.

Did you know that...

Pumpkins are sweet, but don't be fooled: the pulp is actually low in sugar and rich in water (94%), thus favoring the body's purification. It is also particularly rich in antioxidants, vitamins – especially vitamin A, like all orange vegetables, and vitamin C – and minerals, above all potassium, phosphorus, calcium and magnesium. Thanks to its low caloric value, with only 15 calories for every 3 1/2 oz. (100 grams), its good fiber content and a highly satisfying flavor, it is ideal for those who follow a strict diet.

Difficulty

TOMATOES MEDITERRANEAN-STYLE

POMODORI ALLA MEDITERRANEA

Preparation time: 20 minutes + 15 minutes cooking time

4 Servings

1 lb. (500 g) **tomatoes, halved**
  (about 4 medium)
Salt
1 tsp. **chopped fresh parsley**
1 tsp. **chopped fresh basil**
1/2 tsp. **fresh thyme leaves**
1/2 tsp. **fresh oregano**
1/2 tsp. **fresh chopped marjoram**
1 1/4 cups (125 g) **breadcrumbs**
1/4 cup (60 ml) **extra-virgin olive oil**

Method

Place the tomatoes in a colander, sprinkle with salt, and let drain for 15 minutes.

Meanwhile, stir the herbs into the breadcrumbs. Add the oil and mix well.

Heat the oven to 350°F (175°C). Place the tomatoes, cut side up, in a 9-inch (23 cm) baking pan. Spread the breadcrumb mixture on the tomatoes and bake for about 15 minutes, or until golden.

Did you know that...

Basil (Ocimum basilicum) is a worldwide symbol of Italian gastronomy. The herbaceous plant probably originated in India, and tradition says that it was introduced to Europe after Alexander the Great's expedition to that far-off land. Basil gets its name from the Greek word basileùs ("king") and was known to botanists as the "royal herb," perhaps because of its intense and unmistakable flavor. But the name is all that has remained "royal" about this aromatic plant for some time. In ancient times, basil was thought to have many therapeutic properties and its aroma was considered a potent aphrodisiac. Adorning oneself with basil leaves was considered a message of both love and the desire to please. Perhaps that's why Giovanni Boccaccio, in one of the most harrowing novellas of the Decameron, had the desperate Lisabetta bury the head of her lover (who was killed by her brothers) in a pot, from which the young maiden went on to raise a fragrant basil plant with great love and devotion.

Difficulty

EGGPLANT CAPONATA WITH FENNEL, OLIVES, AND RAISINS

CAPONATA CON FINOCCHIO, OLIVE, E UVA PASSA

Preparation time: 30 minutes + 20 minutes cooking time

4 Servings

1 lb. (500 g) **eggplant**
  (about 1 medium)
Salt and freshly ground black pepper
  to taste
3 oz. (100 g) **raisins**
  (about 2/3 cup packed)
8 oz. (200 g) **red onions**
  (about 1 1/2 medium)
14 oz. (400 g) **red bell peppers**
  (about 2 medium)
1 **stalk fennel (bulb and fronds)**
2 **cloves garlic**
12 oz. (300 g) **tomatoes**
  (about 3 small)
1/3 cup (80 ml) **extra-virgin olive oil**
3 oz. (100 g) **black olives, pitted**
  (about 23 large)
3/4 oz. (15 g) **fresh basil leaves**
  (about 30 leaves), plus more
  for garnish
1 tsp. **sugar**
1/3 cup (80 ml) **red-wine vinegar**
1 oz. (30 g) **pine nuts**
  (about 3 1/2 tbsp.)

Method

Dice the eggplant, put it in a colander, salt it lightly, and allow it to drain for about 30 minutes.

Soak the raisins in warm water for 15 minutes, then drain and squeeze out any excess liquid. Chop the fennel fronds and set aside.

Dice the onions, bell peppers, fennel bulb, garlic, and tomatoes. Heat the oil in a large skillet over medium heat and sauté the onions. Add the eggplant, bell peppers, fennel bulb, and garlic and cook until the eggplant softens, about 10 minutes. Add the olives and raisins, and lastly, the tomatoes. Season the vegetables with half of the basil, a pinch of salt, and a generous dash of pepper.

Cover the pan and let the liquid reduce for 5 minutes, stirring occasionally. Add the sugar and vinegar and let it continue cooking, uncovered, until the mixture is dense and the vegetables are tender.

In a heated nonstick pan, lightly toast the pine nuts. Garnish the mixture with the remaining basil, chopped fennel fronds, and toasted pine nuts and serve.

Difficulty

ARTICHOKE SALAD WITH PARMIGIANO REGGIANO

INSALATA DI CARCIOFI CON PARMIGIANO REGGIANO

Preparation time: 20 minutes

4 Servings

4 artichokes

Juice of 2 lemons

3 1/2 tbsp. (50 ml) **extra-virgin olive oil (preferably from Liguria), plus more for drizzling**

Salt and freshly ground black pepper

1 cup plus 3 tbsp. (120 g) **grated Parmigiano Reggiano cheese**

4 to 5 **fresh mint leaves, torn**

Method

Clean the artichokes by slicing at least 1/4 inch (5 mm) off the tops and bottoms and removing all the tough outer leaves. Cut the artichokes in half lengthwise and remove the chokes. Cut into thin slices and soak in a bowl of water with half of the lemon juice to prevent the artichokes from turning black.

Meanwhile, combine the remaining lemon juice, the olive oil, and a pinch of salt and pepper. Drain the artichokes. Drizzle the olive oil mixture over the artichoke slices. Arrange them in the center of the plate. Top with the Parmigiano, mint, and a drizzle of olive oil.

Did you know that...

As Montaigne noted with great surprise in The Journal of Montaigne's Travels in Italy, *from the late sixteenth century, the artichoke* (Cynara scolymus) *is often eaten raw in Italy. Likely derived from the wild cardoon, the Italians' extraordinary agricultural skills and inventive gastronomy led to the exceptional product that we know today. The use of artichokes began to spread in the sixteenth century, and, like all little-known plants, it was immediately assigned symbolic meanings and curious medical and scientific beliefs. For example, the artichoke's reputation as a potent aphrodisiac may be why it was forbidden to young people from good families.*

Difficulty

COUNTRY-STYLE ARTICHOKE PIE
TORTA RUSTICA DI CARCIOFI

Preparation time: 40 minutes + 45 minutes cooking time

4 Servings

FOR THE PASTRY DOUGH

7 oz. (200 g) **all-purpose flour
(about 1 1/3 cups)**

7 oz. (200 g) **fresh ricotta cheese**

1/3 cup plus 1 1/2 tbsp. (100 ml)
extra-virgin olive oil

FOR THE FILLING

12 **artichokes**

1 tbsp. **unsalted butter**

Salt and freshly ground black pepper

3 **large eggs**

1 3/4 oz. (50 g) **Pecorino cheese,
grated**

8 3/4 oz. (250 g) **Parma ham**

2 oz. (60 g) **mozzarella cheese
(about 2 small)**

3 oz. (100 g) **Fontina cheese,
very thinly sliced**

Method

Make the pastry dough: Put the flour on a clean work surface. Gradually incorporate the ricotta and the olive oil to form a soft dough. Divide the dough in half and form into 2 balls. Set aside.

Make the filling: Clean artichokes by slicing at least 1/4 inch (5 mm) off the tops and bottoms and removing all the tough outer leaves. Cut the artichokes in half lengthwise and remove the chokes. Cut into thin slices and soak in a bowl of water with the lemon juice to prevent the artichokes from turning black. Remove any tough internal fibers from the artichokes, and julienne them.

Sauté the artichokes in a large skillet over medium heat with the butter and a pinch of salt and pepper for 10 minutes.

Transfer the artichokes to a large bowl and mix with the eggs and Pecorino.

Dice the Parma ham and the mozzarella finely and add them to the artichoke mixture.

Heat the oven to 400°F (200°C). Roll out the balls of pastry dough into 8 rounds, 1/8 inch (3 mm) thick. Place one round of dough on the bottom of a 9-inch (23 cm) pie plate and place the Fontina on top. Spread the filling evenly over the Fontina. Place the second round of dough over the filling and pinch the edges. Bake for about 45 minutes, or until the top of the pie is golden-brown.

Difficulty

FRIED VEGETABLES
FRITTO DI VERDURE

Preparation time: 30 minutes + 5 minutes cooking time

4 Servings

5 oz. (150 g) zucchini
(about 1 medium)

5 oz. (150 g) bell peppers
(about 2 small)

5 oz. (150 g) eggplant
(about 1/4 large)

5 oz. (150 g) red onions, preferably
Tropea (about 2 small)

1 3/4 oz. (50 g) squash blossoms

Extra-virgin olive oil, for frying

3/4 cup plus 1 1/2 tbsp. (200 ml)
milk

1 2/3 cups (200 g) all-purpose flour

Salt to taste

Method

Clean and peel the vegetables and cut all except the squash blossoms into thin strips. Heat 1 inch (2.5 cm) of oil in a large pot over medium heat until shimmering.

Place the milk in a bowl; place the flour in another bowl. Dip all the vegetables and the whole squash blossoms in the milk. Dredge them in the flour, shake off the excess, and fry them in the oil until golden-brown.

Using a slotted spoon, transfer the vegetables to paper towels to drain. Sprinkle them with salt and serve them very hot.

Did you know that...

Perhaps the most prominent feature of Mediterranean cuisine, particularly Italian cuisine, is the omnipresence of vegetables. Whether they're wild herbs, roots or garden vegetables, the importance of this component is irrefutable. This characteristic was noted by Giacomo Castelvetro, an intellectual and a man of letters who fled to England after being accused of heresy during the Counter-Reformation. Far from his homeland, he missed the use of vegetables and salads in everyday cooking and pondered the reasons why Italians used those items so much. According to Castelvetro, the first reason has to do with the economic nature and production of Italian terrain, which wasn't made for large-scale breeding. The second reason has to do with climate – the heat and sun of the Italian peninsula aren't conducive to consuming large quantities of meat. These objective geomorphological, economic and structural factors influenced individual and collective tastes, which became subjective, symbolic and cultural over time.

Difficulty

RATATOUILLE
RATATOUILLE

Preparation time: 10 minutes + 20 minutes cooking time

4 Servings

1/3 cup plus 1 1/2 tbsp. (100 ml)
  extra-virgin olive oil
1 clove garlic
6 oz. (180 g) red onions
  (about 2 medium), thinly sliced
3 1/2 oz. (100 g) red bell pepper
  (about 1/2 large), cut into 3/4-inch
  (2 cm) dice
3 1/2 oz. (100 g) yellow bell pepper
  (about 1/2 large), cut into 3/4-inch
  (2 cm) dice
7 oz. (200 g) eggplant (about 1/3 large),
  cut into 3/4-inch (2 cm) dice
11 oz. (300 g) zucchini (about
  2 medium), cut into 3/4-inch
  (2 cm) dice
7 oz. (200 g) grape tomatoes, halved
Salt and freshly ground black pepper
  to taste
4 fresh basil leaves, torn

Difficulty

Method

Heat the olive oil in a large pot over medium heat. Add the garlic and the onions and cook until softened, about 5 minutes.

Add the bell peppers and cook for 3 minutes. Add the eggplant and sauté until just tender, about 4 minutes. Add the zucchini. Cook for an additional 5 minutes, then add the tomatoes and season with salt and pepper.

Reduce the heat to medium low, add the basil, and continue to cook for 5 minutes.

Did you know that...

High gastronomy in the Middle Ages, Renaissance and Italian Baroque period assigned great importance to an element that, in a way, has only recently been taken into consideration again – the visual presentation of a dish. But in the Middle Ages, it wasn't just a matter of simple aesthetics. Colors actually had very specific symbolic meanings, and even in a culinary context they were a means to a particular end. They were incorporated through the use of ingredients with naturally bold colors and the addition of precious spices (like saffron) or artificial dyes. Regarding the symbolic meaning of various colors, white was associated with purity and balance, and it's no coincidence that even today in Italy people suffering stomach problems are advised to mangiare in bianco (literally to "eat white food" or follow a diet that's as bland as possible). Red was a symbol of strength, instinct and carnality. Blue was associated with mysticism and ascension. And finally, yellow was the irrefutable king of aristocratic life in the past. As the color of gold and sunlight, it was considered a genuine terrestrial manifestation of the divine.

SWEET-AND-SOUR ZUCCHINI

ZUCCHINE IN AGRODOLCE

Preparation time: 15 minutes + 15 minutes cooking time

4 Servings

2 1/8 oz. (60 g) **sugar (about 1/3 cup)**
1/4 cup (60 ml) **white-wine vinegar**
2 1/4 lbs. (1 kg) **small zucchini**
Vegetable oil, for frying
Salt to taste

Method

Make the sweet-and-sour marinade: In a small frying pan over low heat, dissolve the sugar in the vinegar and keep warm.

Wash the zucchini and cut into rounds 1/4 inch (5 mm) thick. Heat 1/2 inch (1 cm) of oil in a large skillet until shimmering. Fry the zucchini in batches until tender. Using a slotted spoon, transfer the zucchini to paper towels to drain.

Arrange the zucchini in a baking dish. Sprinkle with salt and pour the sweet-and-sour marinade over the top. Serve. (In summer, this dish is also good served cold.)

Difficulty

Did you know that...

Sweet-and-sour sauces can be traced back to the ancient practice of mixing sweet ingredients with more acidic ones to create distinct, intense flavors. Indeed, there are traces of "sweet-and-sour" flavors from Roman times, when honey and vinegar were combined.

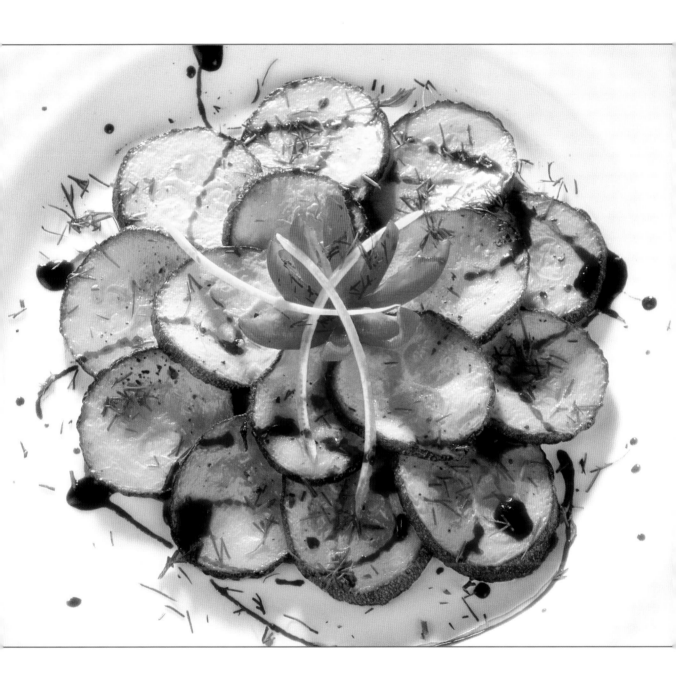

FAVA BEANS WITH ANCHOVIES
FAVE ALLE ACCIUGHE

Preparation time: 10 minutes + 5 minutes cooking time

4 Servings

2 1/4 lbs. (1 kg) **fresh fava beans**
Salt and freshly ground black pepper
  to taste
2 **cloves garlic, chopped**
1 **pinch marjoram**
2 tbsp. (30 ml) **vinegar**
1/4 cup (60 ml) **extra-virgin olive oil**
4 **anchovies, desalted, deboned,**
  and chopped (optional)

Method

Boil the fava beans in a medium pot of salted water until they are *al dente*, about 5 minutes; then drain.

Prepare the sauce: Mix the garlic, marjoram, vinegar, olive oil, and anchovies, if desired. Season with salt and pepper and drizzle over the fava beans.

Alternatively, serve the fava beans with chopped fresh chives, oil, and salt and pepper to taste.

Did you know that...

Though legumes were always eaten in abundance in antiquity, especially by the lower classes, the story of fava beans (vicia fava) is curious and, in some ways, mysterious. The philosopher Pythagoras forbade his disciples to eat them, and admission to the School of Pythagoras, which was active in Magna Graecia at the turn of the 5th century BC, required disciples to conform to some very rigid standards, including dietary regulations; Pythagoras is actually considered the first advocate of vegetarianism in the Western world. But the true reason behind the "fava bean taboo" remains a mystery. It could be the result of a purely physical phenomenon – a genetic disorder that results in a serious physical reaction to repeated consumption of fava beans (called favism) seems particularly common in southern Italy. But it's more likely that this bizarre choice was made for anthropological reasons. As Levi-Strauss already noted, fava beans were often involved in ancient rituals connected to the afterlife, perhaps because they have such a smooth stem. So it's plausible that they were considered "demonic" plants linked to the world of the dead and possessing magic powers of communication with the great beyond. Many centuries have passed since the strange ideas of Pythagoras, and Italian culinary history, which features fava beans in many wonderful recipes, has certainly redefined the bean's image.

Difficulty

ITALIAN WHITE BEANS WITH SAGE
FAGIOLI ALL'UCCELLETTO

Preparation time: 1 hour 20 minutes + 12 hours soaking time + 20 minutes cooking time

4 Servings

14 oz. (400 g) **dried toscanelli or cannellini beans**

Salt and freshly ground black pepper to taste

14 oz. (400 g) **tomatoes (about 4 small)**

3 1/2 tbsp. (50 ml) **extra-virgin olive oil**

2 **cloves garlic**

1 **sprig fresh sage**

Method

Soak the beans in a pot of cold water overnight; drain.

Bring a pot of unsalted water to a boil. Cook the beans for 15 to 20 minutes, until tender yet firm; drain.

Meanwhile, cut an X in the bottom of the tomatoes and blanch in boiling water for 10 to 15 seconds. Plunge in a bowl of ice water, then peel, seed, and dice them.

Heat the oil in a skillet and add the garlic. Add the tomatoes and sauté for 10 minutes. Add the beans, season with salt and pepper, and cook for another 10 minutes. Garnish with whole or chopped sage, as desired.

Did you know that...

When you think about Mediterranean cooking, aromatic herbs are probably one of the first ingredients that come to mind. No other culinary tradition is associated with fresh herbs and fragrances (wild or cultivated) more than Mediterranean cuisine. Though they may seem secondary, a quick look through Medieval and Renaissance cookbooks confirms their gastronomic importance. All that's changed over time is the order and predominance of certain herbs in various recipes. During the Middle Ages and the Renaissance, mint and marjoram were most prevalent, followed by rosemary, parsley, sage and anise. But today basil rules above all, though in the past it occupied a surprisingly marginal position along with bay laurel, catmint and pimpernel.

Difficulty

PARMA-STYLE ASPARAGUS

ASPARAGI ALLA PARMIGIANA

Preparation time: 15 minutes + 10 minutes cooking time

4 Servings

1 3/4 lbs. (800 g) **asparagus**
Salt to taste
1 3/4 oz. (50 g) **Parmigiano Reggiano
cheese, grated (about 1/2 cup)**
4 tbsp. (60 g) **unsalted butter**

Method

Wash the asparagus and trim the stalks to the same length.

Tie them into small bundles and stand them upright in a saucepan of salted water. Boil them, tips upward, until cooked but still firm, about 10 minutes. Drain and arrange on a serving dish. Sprinkle the asparagus tips with the grated Parmigiano.

Meanwhile, melt the butter in a saucepan until frothy. Pour it over the asparagus and serve.

Did you know that...

Asparagus is a spring vegetable, a flowering perennial plant species which possibly originated in Mesopotamia (the name derives from the Persian sperega, *meaning shoot). It was cultivated and used by the Egyptians and by the population of Asia Minor more than 2,000 years ago. The first person to write about asparagus, in a treatise on the history of plants, was the Greek Theophrastus in 300 B.C. A century later, Cato the Roman also wrote about it. And in 79 B.C., his fellow citizen Pliny wrote about asparagus in his* Naturalis Historia, *which illustrates how to cultivate it. Asparagus was indeed very popular with the Ancient Romans, both because of the culinary qualities that make it a true delicacy, and for its medicinal properties: it has a purifying effect on the kidneys and analgesic properties for toothache. Today, various types of asparagus are cultivated for culinary purposes. They differ in appearance, flavor and cultivation methods. For example, the White Asparagus of Bassano del Grappa, which owes its color to the fact that it is cultivated in the absence of light to block natural photosynthesis. The age-old Purple Asparagus of Albenga is bright purple and relatively large in size. The Pink Asparagus of Mezzago, the color of whose tips is due to very few hours of exposure to sunlight before picking, or the prized Green Asparagus of Altedo cultivated in the provinces of Bologna and Ferrara.*

Difficulty

BAKED STUFFED VEGETABLES
VERDURE RIPIENE AL FORNO

Preparation time: 30 minutes + 30 minutes cooking time

4 Servings

14 oz. (400 g) **zucchini (about 2 large)**

1 lb. (500 g) **tomatoes
(about 4 medium)**

5 oz. (150 g) **yellow bell peppers
(about 2 small)**

3 1/2 tbsp. (50 ml) **extra-virgin
olive oil**

1/4 lb. (100 g) **ground beef**

**Salt and freshly ground black pepper
to taste**

2 **large eggs, lightly beaten**

1 3/4 oz. (50 g) **Parmigiano Reggiano
cheese, grated (about 1/2 cup)**

1 3/4 oz. (50 g) **fresh breadcrumbs
(about 1/3 cup)**

Ground nutmeg

Method

Wash the zucchini and trim off the ends. In a medium pot fitted with a vegetable steamer, steam the zucchini until just tender, about 8 minutes. Cut them lengthwise, seed them, and scrape out the flesh with a teaspoon or melon baller. Chop the zucchini pulp and set aside. Also set aside the zucchini shells.

Remove the stems from the tomatoes, cut off the tops, and scoop out the pulp. Chop the tomato pulp and set aside the tomato shells and the pulp.

Halve the bell peppers, removing the seeds and ribs.

Heat half of the oil in a large skillet, add the ground beef, and sauté until browned. Add the zucchini and the tomato pulp and cook for a few minutes to evaporate the excess liquid. Season with salt and pepper.

Heat the oven to 350°F (175°C). Transfer the ground-beef mixture to a bowl and set aside to cool. When it is cool, add the eggs, half of the grated Parmigiano, and the breadcrumbs. Season with the salt and pepper and a pinch of nutmeg. Stir to combine.

Fill the zucchini and tomato shells with the ground-beef mixture using a spoon or a pastry bag. Transfer stuffed vegetables to a greased baking sheet and sprinkle with the remaining Parmigiano and a drop of olive oil.

Bake in the oven for about 30 minutes, or until golden-brown. Serve the baked stuffed vegetables hot or cold, as desired.

Difficulty

VEGETABLES AU GRATIN
VERDURE GRATINATE

Preparation time: 30 minutes + 20 minutes cooking time

4 Servings

FOR THE VEGETABLES

5 oz. (150 g) **cauliflower florets**
5 oz. (150 g) **leek, white part only
(about 1 small)**
5 oz. (150 g) **Brussels sprouts**
Salt

FOR THE BÉCHAMEL

4 tbsp. (60 g) **unsalted butter,
plus more for drizzling**
1/3 cup (40 g) **all-purpose flour**
2 cups (1/2 l) **milk**
Salt to taste
Fresh nutmeg to taste
1 3/4 oz. (50 g) **Parmigiano Reggiano
cheese, grated (about 1/2 cup)**

Method

Rinse the cauliflower, leeks, and Brussels sprouts. Remove and discard the roots and green parts of the leeks and the wilted outer leaves of the Brussels sprouts.

Boil the vegetables separately in salted water until they can be easily pierced with a knife. Drain and let them cool.

Make the béchamel: Melt the butter in a heavy-bottomed pan. To make a roux, add the flour and whisk it and the butter together for 3 to 4 minutes over low heat, until smooth.

Heat the milk in a separate pan, then add to the roux, pouring it in a slow stream. Adjust the salt and continue cooking, whisking constantly to avoid the formation of lumps, until the sauce is thick and creamy. If the béchamel is too thick, add a bit of milk. If it is too thin, let it cook for a few additional minutes. Season with salt and a grating of nutmeg.

Heat the oven to 350°F (175°C). Grease four ramekins (or a single baking dish, especially for leeks) with the remaining butter. Place the vegetables (together or separate, as you desire) in the baking dishes and pour béchamel over them. Sprinkle with Parmigiano and drizzle with a little melted butter.

Roast the vegetables for 20 minutes, or until a golden crust forms.

Difficulty

DESSERTS

CHAPTER SEVEN

RICOTTA MOUSSE WITH ALMOND MILK

SPUMA DI RICOTTA AL LATTE DI MANDORLA

Preparation time: 1 hour + 8 hours resting time + 3 hours freezing time

4 Servings

FOR THE ALMOND MILK

3 1/2 oz. (100 g) **unsalted almonds,
   finely ground (about 1 cup)**
1 1/4 cups (300 ml) **water**

2 **large egg yolks**
1/4 cup plus 2 tbsp. (75 g) **sugar**
2 **gelatin sheets (5 g)**
   or 1/2 **envelope granulated
   gelatin (1/8 oz.), optional**
9 oz. (250 g) **fresh ricotta cheese**
2/3 cup (160 ml) **fresh cream**

Method

Make almond milk: Mix the ground almonds with the water and refrigerate the mixture for 8 hours. Strain the almond milk through cheesecloth.

Beat the egg yolks with the sugar and stir in 1/2 cup (125 ml) of the almond milk. Transfer to a medium pan over medium heat and let the mixture thicken, stirring occasionally.

If you are using gelatin sheets, soak them in water until softened; squeeze out any excess water. Dissolve the gelatin in the hot almond-milk mixture. Let the mixture cool and stir in the ricotta.

In a bowl, whip the cream and fold it into the ricotta mixture. Pour into individual dessert molds and freeze for about 3 hours. Unmold and serve chilled.

Difficulty

ANGEL WINGS
CHIACCHIERE

Preparation time: 30 minutes + 30 minutes resting time + 3 minutes cooking time

4 Servings

2 cups (250 g) **all-purpose flour**
1/3 tsp. (1.5 g) **baking powder**
Salt
1 **large egg**
1 1/2 tbsp. (25 g) **unsalted butter,**
  melted and cooled
2 1/2 tbsp. (20 g) **confectioners' sugar,**
  plus more for dusting
1 tbsp. (15 ml) **grappa**
3 1/2 tbsp. (50 ml) **milk**
1 tsp. (5 ml) **vanilla extract**
Zest of 1/2 lemon, grated
Vegetable oil, for frying
  and for plastic wrap

Method

Sift together the flour, baking powder, and a pinch of salt into a large bowl.

In another large bowl, whisk together the egg, butter, 2 1/2 tablespoons confectioners' sugar, grappa, milk, vanilla, and lemon zest. Gradually add the flour mixture to the egg mixture, kneading until the dough is smooth. Form the dough into a ball, cover with lightly oiled plastic wrap, and let it rest for at least 30 minutes.

On a clean work surface (or using a pasta machine), roll the dough out into thin sheets, about 1/8 inch (3 mm) thick. Cut the pastry into rectangles or diamond shapes with a pastry cutter. To obtain the characteristic wing shape, make three incisions lengthwise in each pastry rectangle or diamond. Fold the upper corner of the rectangle (or the upper corner of the diamond) and insert it into the center incision.

Heat about 1 inch (2.5 cm) of vegetable oil in a large pot until shimmering. Fry the dough for about 3 minutes and drain it on paper towels. Dust with confectioners' sugar before serving.

Did you know that...

Carnival sweets are known by an infinite number of regional names: Chiacchiere, Frappe, cenci, bugie, galani, crostoli, fiocchetti, guanti, intrigoni, lattughe, risole, stracci, pampuglie, and many more. They can have different shapes, depending on how the sheets of pastry are cut: from rough rectangles to elegant ribbons of different lengths, plain or tied in various ways. And they can be dusted with confectioners' sugar, but also covered with honey or chocolate, sprinkled with sweet liqueurs like Alchermes, and served by themselves or with sweetened whipped mascarpone. Chiacchiere are pretty, tempting sweets. This is partly due to their puffed, golden appearance and partly to the magic of frying, which gives them a crisp yet flaky texture.

Difficulty

ORANGE GRANITA
GRANITA ALL'ARANCIA

Preparation time: 15 minutes + 5 to 6 hours freezing time

4 Servings

2 **oranges**
1 cup (250 ml) **water**
1/4 cup plus 2 tbsp. (75 g) **sugar**
3 1/2 tbsp. (50 ml) **lemon juice**

Method

Rinse and zest the oranges. Grate the zest, being careful not to include any of the bitter white pith. Juice the oranges, filtering the juice with a fine-mesh strainer.

Make a syrup by boiling the water and sugar in a small pot for 4 to 5 minutes. Let it cool and combine it with the citrus juices and orange zest, reserving some for garnish, if desired.

Freeze the liquid in an airtight container for about 1 hour, until ice crystals start to form. Whisk it well and return it to the freezer. Repeat this process at least 4 or 5 times. The granita is ready when the ice reaches a uniform consistency and granularity.

Garnish with orange zest, if desired, and serve in dessert bowls.

Did you know that...

Many gastronomic inventions were born from the magical fusion of two traditions. Such is the case of the Sicilian granita. The taste for ice water infused with fruits and flowers was typical of both the Roman and Arabic civilizations, and it found fertile ground in the rich and fragrant island of Sicily. Muslim populations contributed greatly to this process, as they were highly skilled in sugarcane cultivation and production, which was essential for making the syrup that is the base of the granita recipe. The wide availability of juicy, tasty citrus fruits did the rest. Vincenzo Agnoletti, who wrote various treatises on making confections, pastries, and liqueurs in the early nineteenth century, defined this recipe as sorbetto granito, or "grainy sorbet."

Difficulty

GLAZED HAZELNUT COOKIES

BISCOTTI GLASSATI ALLA NOCCIOLA

Preparation time: 30 minutes + 2 hours resting time + 10 to 12 minutes cooking time

4 to 6 Servings

FOR THE DOUGH

2/3 cup (150 g) **unsalted butter, softened at room temperature**

1 cup plus 2 tsp. (125 g) **confectioners' sugar**

1 **large egg**

Zest of 1 lemon, grated

Vanilla extract

2 1/2 cups (300 g) **all-purpose flour, plus more for dusting**

3/4 tsp. (2 1/2g) **baking powder**

Salt

3/4 cup (100 g) **whole hazelnuts, toasted and ground into flour**

FOR THE GLAZE

1 **large egg white**

2/3 cup (120 g) **sugar**

3 3/4 tsp. (10 g) **cornstarch**

All-purpose flour for dusting

Confectioners' sugar

Method

Make the dough: With an electric mixer on medium-high speed, cream the butter with the confectioners' sugar.

Add the egg, lemon zest, and a dash of vanilla.

Sift together the flour, the baking powder, a pinch of salt, and the hazelnut flour and combine with the butter mixture. Knead for a few minutes.

Form the dough into a ball, wrap in plastic wrap, and refrigerate for at least 1 hour.

Make the glaze: Beat the egg white with the sugar until the mixture is light and fluffy. Add the cornstarch and beat to combine.

On a clean, lightly floured work surface, roll out the dough to between 1/8 and 1/4 inch (4 mm) thick. Place the dough on a parchment-lined surface. Spread the glaze over the dough and let sit for 1 hour.

Heat the oven to 350°F (175°C).

Cut out the cookies in any shape you desire and arrange on a parchment-lined baking sheet. Bake for 10 to 12 minutes.

Difficulty

LADY'S KISSES

BACI DI DAMA

Preparation time: 40 minutes + 30 minutes resting time + 15 minutes cooking time

4 Servings

3/4 cup (100 g) **roasted hazelnuts**
1/4 cup (25 g) **blanched almonds**
1/2 cup plus 2 tbsp. (125 g) **sugar**
1/2 cup (125 g) **unsalted butter,
softened at room temperature,
plus more for baking sheet**
1 cup (125 g) **all-purpose flour,
plus more for dusting**
3/8 cup (30 g) **unsweetened cocoa
powder**
3 1/2 oz. (100 g) **dark chocolate**

Method

In a blender or food processor, pulse the hazelnuts and almonds with the sugar until finely ground.

In a bowl, combine the hazelnut mixture with the butter.

In another bowl, sift together the flour and cocoa, then stir it into the butter mixture just until incorporated.

Wrap the mixture in plastic wrap and refrigerate for at least 30 minutes.

Heat the oven to 325°F (160°C).

On a clean, lightly floured work surface, roll out the chilled mixture to a thickness of about 3/8 inch (1 cm). Cut out disks with pastry rings 5/8 to 3/4 inch (1.5 to 2 cm) in diameter and shape into balls.

Arrange the balls on a lightly buttered, floured (or parchment-lined) baking sheet. Bake for 15 minutes.

Let cool completely, then transfer, rounded side down, to a wire rack.

Meanwhile, melt the chocolate in a heatproof bowl set over (not in) a pan of simmering water, or in the microwave. Let it cool until it begins to crystallize.

Pour a little on melted chocolate each of half the batch of cookies. Place the flatter side of another cookie on top of each and allow the lady's kisses to set for 30 minutes.

Difficulty

CHOCOLATE-COATED FIGS
FICHI AL CIOCCOLATO

Preparation time: 20 minutes + 5 minutes cooking time

4 Servings

1 3/4 lbs. (800 g) **dried figs**
5 oz. (150 g) **almonds, toasted
and chopped**
2 **cloves, crushed**
3 oz. (70 g) **candied citron**
3 1/2 oz. (100 g) **dark chocolate,
grated**
1/4 cup plus 2 tbsp. (75 g) **sugar**
Ground cinnamon (optional)

Method

Heat the oven to 350°F (175°C).

With a sharp knife, slice into each fig from top to bottom—following the line of the stem—splitting it but leaving the split halves still attached. Fold open each fig like a book, exposing the cut surfaces, and top each half with some of the almonds, cloves, and candied citron. Close them firmly, place on a parchment-lined baking sheet, and bake until they begin to brown, about 5 minutes.

Meanwhile, in a bowl, mix the chocolate and sugar. While the figs are still hot, roll them in the chocolate mixture. (Alternatively, you can melt the chocolate with a little water and a pinch of cinnamon in a baking dish, then dip the hot figs in the cinnamon-chocolate.) Place the figs on a parchment-lined baking sheet to set.

Store the chocolate-coated figs in tins or wooden boxes lined with waxed paper.

Difficulty

TIRAMISÙ

TIRAMISÙ

Preparation time: 30 minutes + 2 hours resting time

4 Servings

4 large egg yolks
  plus 2 large egg whites
1/2 cup plus 2 tbsp. (125 g) **sugar**
1 cup (250 g) **mascarpone**
8 ladyfingers
1 cup (200 ml) **sweetened coffee**
1 tbsp. plus 2 tsp. (25 ml) **brandy**
  (optional)
Unsweetened cocoa powder,
  as needed

Method

Beat the egg yolks with 1/4 cup plus 1 tablespoon (60 g) of the sugar in a heatproof bowl until thick and pale, then set over (not in) a pan of simmering water until warmed through. Remove from the heat.

In another bowl, beat the egg whites with the remaining sugar until stiff peaks form.

Stir the mascarpone and brandy into the egg yolk mixture, then gently fold in the egg white mixture, letting it remain light and frothy.

If using the brandy, add it to the sweetened coffee. Dip the ladyfingers into the coffee. Transfer 4 ladyfingers to an 8-inch (20 cm) glass baking dish or 4 small dessert bowls.

Pour in a layer of the cream mixture, alternating with another layer of the ladyfingers and ending with the cream.

Refrigerate the tiramisù, covered, for about 2 hours.

Top with a generous dusting of the cocoa.

Difficulty

FROZEN ZABAGLIONE WITH MOSCATO D'ASTI PASSITO AND MELON PURÉE

ZABAIONE GELATO AL MOSCATO D'ASTI PASSITO SU FRULLATO DI MELONE

Preparation time: 15 minutes + 2 hours resting time + 10 minutes cooking time

4 Servings

FOR THE ZABAGLIONE
6 large egg yolks
1 cup (200 g) sugar
3/4 cup (200 ml) Moscato d'Asti
 or other Muscat wine
8 1/3 cups (500 g) whipped cream

FOR THE MELON PURÉE
1 melon (such as cantaloupe),
 peeled, seeded, and cut into chunks
1/4 cup (50 g) sugar

Method

Make the zabaglione: Whisk together the egg yolks and the sugar in a copper pan or a heatproof bowl until frothy. Transfer the egg mixture to a copper pot or place the heatproof bowl over (not in) a pan of simmering water over medium-low heat. Slowly add the Moscato to the egg mixture, whisking constantly.

Bring the zabaglione to 175°F (80°C) on a candy or instant-read thermometer. When it begins to thicken, remove from the heat and let cool.

Gently fold in the whipped cream. Pour the mixture into a medium heatproof bowl and refrigerate for 2 hours.

Make the melon purée: Use a blender or food processor to purée the melon with the sugar.

To serve, remove the zabaglione from the bowl. Ladle the purée into each dessert dish and arrange thin slices of the zabaglione on top.

Difficulty

CRÈME CARAMEL
CRÈME CARAMEL

Preparation time: 15 minutes + 2 hours resting time + 35 to 40 minutes cooking time

4 Servings

FOR THE CARAMEL
1/4 cup (50 g) **sugar**
1 tbsp. (15 ml) **water**

FOR THE CUSTARD
1 1/3 cups (330 ml) **milk**
3/8 cup (85 g) **sugar**
Zest of 1/2 lemon
2 **large eggs, beaten**

Method

Make the caramel: In a saucepan over medium-high heat, combine the sugar and the water and bring to a boil. Reduce the heat to medium and cook until the mixture is light brown and caramelized. Divide the caramel evenly between 4 ramekins or small dessert molds, swirling to coat the ramekins. Let cool.

Make the custard: In a saucepan, combine the milk, sugar, and lemon zest and bring to a boil. Remove and discard the zest.

In a bowl, combine a quarter of the milk mixture and the eggs and stir well. Add the remaining milk mixture. (This will help you avoid cooking the eggs.) Pour the mixture into the ramekins.

Prepare a hot water bath (bain-marie): Place the ramekins in a deep baking pan. Fill the pan with enough hot water to reach halfway up the sides of the ramekins. Bake until the custards are firm in the centers, 35 to 40 minutes.

Transfer the ramekins to a wire cooling rack, cool completely, then refrigerate for at least 2 hours.

Before serving, run a knife around the edge of each ramekin and invert onto a dessert plate; unmold the crème with the caramel on top.

Difficulty

ALPHABETICAL INDEX OF RECIPES

INGREDIENTS INDEX

All photographs are by
ACADEMIA BARILLA

In the heart of Parma, one of the most distinguished capitals of Italian cuisine, is the Barilla Center. Set on the grounds of the former Barilla pasta factory, this modern architectural complex is the home of Academia Barilla. This was founded in 2004 to promote the art of Italian cuisine, protecting the regional gastronomic heritage and safeguarding it from imitations and counterfeits, while encouraging the great traditions of the Italian restaurant industry. Academia Barilla is also a center of great professionalism and talent that is exceptional in the world of cooking. It organizes cooking classes for culinary enthusiasts, it provides services for those involved in the restaurant industry, and it offers products of the highest quality. In 2007, Academia Barilla was awarded the "Premio Impresa-Cultura" for its campaigns promoting the culture and creativity of Italian gastronomy throughout the world. The center was designed to meet the training requirements of the world of food and it is equipped with all the multimedia facilities necessary for organizing major events. The remarkable gastronomic auditorium is surrounded by a restaurant, a laboratory for sensory analysis, and various teaching rooms equipped with the most modern technology. The Gastronomic Library contains over 11,000 books and a an impressive collection of historic menus as well as prints related to culinary subjects. The vast cultural heritage of the library can be consulted on the internet, which provides access to hundreds of digitized historic texts. This avant-garde approach and the presence of a team of internationally famous experts enables Academia Barilla to offer a wide range of courses, meeting the needs of both restaurant chefs and amateur food lovers. In addition, Academia Barilla arranges cultural events and activities aiming to develop the art of cooking, supervised by experts, chefs, and food critics, that are open to the public. It also organizes the "Academia Barilla Film Award" for short films devoted to Italy's culinary traditions.

www.academiabarilla.com

METRIC EQUIVALENTS

| LIQUID/DRY MEASURES ||
U.S.	METRIC
¼ teaspoon	1.25 milliliters
½ teaspoon	2.5 milliliters
1 teaspoon	5 milliliters
1 tablespoon (3 teaspoons)	15 milliliters
1 fluid ounce (2 tablespoons)	30 milliliters
¼ cup	60 milliliters
⅓ cup	80 milliliters
½ cup	120 milliliters
1 cup	240 milliliters
1 pint (2 cups)	480 milliliters
1 quart (4 cups; 32 ounces)	960 milliliters
1 gallon (4 quarts)	3.84 liters
1 ounce (by weight)	28 grams
1 pound	454 grams
2.2 pounds	1 kilogram

OVEN TEMPERATURES

°F	GAS MARK	°C
250	½	120
275	1	140
300	2	150
325	3	165
350	4	180
375	5	190
400	6	200
425	7	220
450	8	230
475	9	240
500	10	260
550	Broil	290